15

36

Mountaineering

Mountaineering

a manual

for

teachers & instructors

D. T. Roscoe

Faber & Faber
3 Queen Square London

First published in 1976
by Faber and Faber Limited
3 Queen Square London WC1
Printed in Great Britain by
Cox & Wyman Ltd, Fakenham

ISBN 0 571 09456 2

Contents

Acknowledgements

I wish to express my thanks to Colin Mortlock, Tom Price, Colonel J. M. Adam, John Wright & Sons Ltd., and *Mountain Magazine* for their permission to print extracts from their works. I am indebted to all who have helped me with advice and information and in particular to Dr Ieuan Jones for his guidance in the First Aid section, Mr P. J. E. Madge for his preparation of much of the photographic material and Miss Barbara Spark for her painstaking work in checking the manuscript and proofs.

D.T.R.

Foreword

In Britain there are many and varied reasons why there is an increase in the number of those taking part in outdoor recreation. Some of these are the growth of leisure time, higher wages, longer holidays and evidence of an increasing desire to be active participants rather than passive watchers. There is the influence of magazines, books, television spectaculars and certainly a growing reaction from the industrial urban life of the twentieth century and a need for the physical and mental refreshment gained out of doors.

Many youth leaders, teachers, centre instructors, club members and other interested adults introduce parties of young people to the mountains and the moorlands. The more experienced they are the better they do it.

This book is about mountain days and how best to show people the way to the mountains. The author is very experienced and highly qualified to write the book. For many years he has been an active mountaineer in Britain, the Alps and south-east Greenland. In addition he was for many years a senior member of my staff at the Plas y Brenin National Mountaineering Centre and there made real impact on the methods of training people in all aspects of mountaineering. At the present time he is Lecturer in Outdoor Education at the University College of North Wales.

This book fills an important need for hitherto there has not been a manual that deals with the instructional or teaching approach, and it will prove of great value to many who care about what they do and how it is done.

It gives me much personal satisfaction to write this short foreword for a book that I am sure is going to help many to introduce others to the hills, where they may find mental and physical refreshment.

John Jackson
Director
Plas y Brenin National Mountaineering Centre

Introduction

In the last decade the numbers of people seeking sport and relaxation in the mountains of the British Isles have increased enormously. Improved travel facilities have made access easier and increased leisure has encouraged more people to seek some form of outdoor activity to enable them to escape from the urban environment for a while. Outdoor activities now form an integral part of the curriculum of many schools and a large number of Local Education Authorities have residential centres in mountain areas. Consequently there is an ever-increasing demand for instruction in mountaineering at both basic and advanced levels. The days when this demand could be met by utilizing the services of an expert friend or clubmate are long gone. The demands are now too great to be met in this way and the need is for teachers and instructors with a sound technical background and a feeling for mountains coupled with teaching ability and experience.

Although there are numerous textbooks dealing with the technical aspects of mountaineering there are very few which deal with any of the teaching aspects or which offer any information useful to the teacher or instructor. It is hoped that this book will go some way towards providing this information both for those working in isolation, perhaps trying to establish mountaineering in a school, and for those working in mountain centres who intend to gain the Mountaineering Instructor's Certificate.

I have not attempted to cover the whole range of topics which one associates with the teaching of mountaineering but have concentrated on aspects in which there is a particular lack of relevant, up-to-date teaching information. The emphasis is on methods and situations which may arise in the teaching of skills rather than on techniques, except in areas such as rope handling where, due to the many possible variations, great confusion still exists and there is a real need for an acceptable teaching system to be established.

I cannot emphasize too strongly the fact that the teaching methods given are by no means the only way in which any particular aspect of the work may be approached. They are proven methods but are intended to be a guide and stimulus rather than an example to be slavishly followed. Originality and spontaneity, coupled with a sound technical background and an awareness of the needs of the students, are among the keynotes to success in teaching outdoor activities of any kind. I would further stress that rules and regulations are not intended to curtail the freedom of choice of the individual mountaineer but should be seen as a guide-line for those in charge of organized groups undergoing instruction. The majority of rules in mountaineering are based upon common sense and the experienced instructor and teacher should be in a position to evaluate and modify them in accordance with the needs of his party, his own expertise and the situation in which he works.

The field of mountaineering teaching is part of the rapidly developing area of outdoor education. Traditional teaching methods are constantly being modified as the needs of the pupils and the criteria governing their development are more clearly seen. This book has been written in the hope that it will contribute in some small measure towards the continuing improvement in teaching standards, but if it merely serves to focus attention on some of the problems and stimulates constructive thought and discussion among those engaged in this area of teaching one of its aims will have been achieved.

Chapter One

Basic Rock Climbing

The approach to rock climbing instruction will vary considerably according to the aims of the teacher, the needs of the students and the teaching situation. A teacher running a school-based club with progression over a period of perhaps two years should, for example, have a completely different approach to that of a mountain centre which has students for one week. Despite these differences, which will be discussed later, certain things will be common to all programmes (with the possible exception of very short 'taster' courses) as they form the basis of the activity. A knowledge of equipment and its correct use, the essentials of movement on rock and a sound system of rope handling are essential to all who might afterwards go away to pursue the activity by themselves.

Equipment

Without the correct equipment in good condition even the best of rock climbers will be potentially unsafe. Centre equipment of any kind is subject to hard usage by novices and should be checked regularly for wear and damage. The choice and care of equipment for instructional use will be dealt with more fully later but it should be stressed that the condition of the equipment is the responsibility of the instructor in charge of rock climbing. Regular checking, maintenance and, if necessary, renewal is essential both from a safety angle and as an example to the students of the standards of equipment which are desirable.

The student has to be taught to respect his equipment and to treat it accordingly. Although he quickly realizes that his life may depend upon the rope, he may tread upon it repeatedly because he knows nothing of the damage which may be caused in this way and he may be absorbed in the technicalities of what he is doing to the exclusion of all else. Even the beginner, receiving a short introduction to the sport, should be given instruction, usually indirectly, in the care of the equipment which he is using. The student who develops an interest in rock climbing needs to know what sort of equipment to buy and how to check and maintain it. This need not be done during a climbing session when the more practical work that takes place the better, but could form the basis of an evening session.

Movement on Rock

Without a doubt the safest climber is he who never falls off. The leader is, or should be, very much aware of this and all his endeavour is directed to getting to the top of the climb with complete control and mastery of the situation. His personal safety factors depend upon the perfection of his technique, and knowledge of his ability and limitations under all conditions. Absolute confidence in his own ability is the hall-mark of the good climber but even the best can miscalculate or be hit by a falling stone. When this happens the climber is forced to rely on his ropework to save him from harm.

When dealing with novices it is impossible to train them to a high standard of personal performance during the course of a week or two. We can and do introduce them to the necessary techniques and present them with a variety of situations where these may be brought into play, but sound movement on rock is a combination of technique, ability and experience. Neither of the last two can be taught or provided on a short course. Sufficient experience to become a sound climber can only be gained over a considerable period of time. I would consider twelve months to be a minimum in this respect. Therefore one of the main objects should be to teach the motivated novice good ropework and modern methods of protection so that he will gain a sound knowledge of the techniques which will safeguard him while gaining further experience should he wish to pursue the sport further.

Ropework

All modern systems of ropework used in the British Isles are variations of the Tarbuck system, based on the Wexler theories, and designed specifically to deal with the problems of handling nylon ropes. A great deal has been written on the classic Tarbuck method and it is assumed that readers of this book will be familiar with its advantages and disadvantages. Briefly these are as follows:

Advantages
i The Tarbuck knot is the strongest of all knots, being virtually as strong as a splice, reducing the strength of the rope by only 20 per cent as opposed to approximately 35 per cent for all other commonly used knots.

ii The waist belay is highly efficient and an inexperienced climber stands a much greater chance of holding a fall using this method than any other method not involving mechanical belaying devices.

iii The waistline distributes the shock of a fall over a greater area of the body than a direct tie thus reducing the chances of internal injury.

iv The belay tension is easily adjusted.

v It is possible to free oneself quickly from the system in an emergency.

Disadvantages
i The knot is complicated, difficult to tie correctly and easily works loose. It should never be tied in a kernmantel rope due to the fact that kernmantel cannot be bent into a loop much smaller than its own diameter which makes it virtually impossible to tie a Tarbuck knot tightly.

ii The hemp waistline is prone to rotting and has to be renewed frequently.

iii The waistline and karabiner are extra links in the safety chain at which failure could occur.

iv It is not so efficient as a direct tie for aid climbing.

v It is a fairly complicated system to learn.

The ideal system should be easy to learn, efficient, pleasant to use in practice and safe in any emergency. For instructional purposes ease of learning is of great importance for, with limited time at our disposal, it would be useless to attempt to teach a system so complicated that it could not be grasped by the average student in a week.

It has long been realized that not all systems and combinations of systems taught in this country are really suitable for novices but until recently each mountain centre taught what it thought to be best and no attempt was made to standardize any particular method. With the advent of the Mountaineering Instructor's Certificate (M.I.C.) it was realized that there was a need for a nationally accepted system so that candidates would know what was required of them in the way of rope-work and so that, it was hoped, some standardization of teaching systems throughout the country would be achieved. During the first M.I.C. assessment course held in November 1968 at the National Mountaineering Centre, Plas y Brenin, both the Tarbuck and Bowline systems (the latter being still in common use at that time) were closely examined in the light of instructing experience, and much practical work was put in on the drop-testing machine in attempts to clarify various arguments. The following major conclusions were reached.

i The waist belay is superior to the shoulder belay in that an un-practised user stands much more chance of successfully arresting a fall and also the rope cannot be lost as in the case of a shoulder belay where the belaying climber can be bent forward by the strain allowing the rope to slip over his head.

ii The disadvantages of the Tarbuck knot far outweigh its advantages and it should be superseded by the figure eight knot. The latter is easy to tie and has a great advantage for novices over all other climbing knots in that mistakes in tying result either in a knot which though incorrect is still sound or no knot at all.

iii The knot strength of both figure eight knots and Bowlines although theoretically weak (about 65 per cent of the rope strength) is acceptable in practice.

iv The waist rope in the Bowline system can be adequately protected by a canvas sheath when used in conjunction with a waist belay.

v Gloves should be worn at all times when belaying.

vi The shoulder belay can be more efficient than the waist one for giving the second man a pull.

With these points in mind Don Roscoe and Ron James worked out a system which was acceptable for M.I.C. rock climbing. It was hoped that this system would also be acceptable to mountain centres, schools and other organizations involved in the teaching of rock climbing. This system has since undergone some modification, particularly with respect to waist ties as a result of the advent of harnesses and belts. As described below it is completely acceptable for M.I.C. rock climbing assessment and is used, with slight variations according to preference and require-ments, by the majority of mountain centres and indeed of climbers in general. Candidates for M.I.C. should ensure that they have a complete understanding of the theory and practice of this system and that they are fluent in its use.

The M.I.C. Rope Handling System

1. Equipment

Rope: No. 4 laid nylon (BS 3104) or 11 mm kernmantel to U.I.A.A. standard. (Union Internationale des Associations d'Alpinisme: the international body which defines standards for mountaineering equipment.)

Gloves: Any glove with a long wrist and good, protective qualities is suitable. Thin leather gloves, while allowing a good grip on the rope, transmit heat readily and are unsuitable. Very thick leather gloves give protection but do not allow a good grip on the rope. The answer seems to lie with ski gloves, which are expensive, good woollen gloves with thin leather stitched on the palms or string gloves.

Crash Helmets: These should be worn at all times including abseiling, mountain rescue practice and descents from cliffs.

Waist Tie: Either a Troll or Irvine/Moac belt and a steel screwgate karabiner to U.I.A.A. specification. (Stubai 5000 or similar.)

Belay Slings: 11 mm or double 9 mm kernmantel. No. 4 or double No. 3 laid nylon. The use of tape for belaying is only to be recommended in situations where it is not possible to use a rope sling. Due to the method of construction it is more easily damaged than rope and can pull through an extremely narrow gap in an apparently sound thread anchor.

Belay Karabiners: As for waist tie.

2. Technique

I. End Tie

A figure eight knot, with the end secured by a tuck back or a full hitch, clipped into the waist karabiner (Pl. 1). This is the simplest method for use by children and beginners. Some people eliminate the karabiner and 'D' ring and tie direct into the belt which eliminates one link of the safety chain. As each link is a potential weakness this is good from the safety aspect but a little more complicated to tie and rather less flexible

in its use for instructional purposes. It is not possible to use this variation with the Irvine belt as the karabiner must be used to secure the belt
around the waist.

II. Middleman's Tie

As for the end tie with the exception that if two ropes are in use the rope
between middle and end man is clipped into a second karabiner attached
directly to the belt.

III. Belaying

Spike Anchors: The rope may be passed either directly round the
anchor or clipped into a karabiner connected to the anchor with a
suitable sling. It is then returned to the waist karabiner through which
a bight is passed. This bight is used to secure the two ropes which form
it using a figure eight knot, i.e. the rope with the end tie is excluded
(Pl. 2a and 2b). When working with children some mountain centres
prefer to teach them to tie a figure eight knot directly into the rope
returning to the waist from the anchor and to clip this into a second
karabiner. This is somewhat more difficult to adjust to obtain the correct
belay tension but has the great advantage for children that should they
untie the wrong knot they will remain safely tied to the rope although
there may be a long trailing 'tail'.

Thread Anchors: The only really satisfactory way of belaying to a
thread anchor is to thread a sling around the anchor, securing the ends
with a screwgate karabiner. The rope is then clipped into the karabiner
and secured as for a spike anchor (Pl. 3). There are several ways of
dealing with the situation where a sling is not available but all have
disadvantages compared with the above method. The simplest is to
untie and thread the climbing rope around the anchor before tying
back in the normal way. This has obvious dangers and should only be
used in really safe situations where there is no possibility of a fall while
unroped. This method should not be used in a teaching situation as it
negates the principle of not untying from the main rope while on the
climb and the conditions of its use demand better judgement and more
experience than a novice can be expected to have. The other main
method of dealing with the situation is complex, wasteful of rope and
difficult to adjust. The belay is made by passing a bight of rope around
the anchor, securing this with a figure eight knot to the waist karabiner

and then securing the live rope from the anchor to the waist with another figure eight knot preferably attached to another karabiner to relieve congestion (Pl. 4a and 4b).

When using the variation end tie all belay knots will of course have to be tied directly into the waistbelt. In theory one then has nylon running over nylon if a waist belay is used but in practice this does not occur. Observation of many falling situations has shown that even with the waistbelt pulled uncomfortably tight the force exerted by a falling climber pulls the belt away from the waist at the point where the ropes are attached. The same force causes the live rope to dig into the waist of the belayer with the result that friction only occurs on the belt and body and *not* on the ropes tied into the belt.

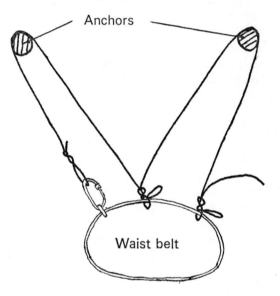

Anchors

Waist belt

FIG. I

If circumstances are such that the karabiner of the belay sling can be clipped direct into the waistbelt without resulting in a slack belay this is quite acceptable, and it is also fast and simple. When doing this one should ensure that the karabiner lies with the gate downwards so that any strain imparted by the waist belay will come on to the back bar. Should it prove necessary to free oneself from the system it can be more difficult to do so when belaying in this way.

When belaying, two separate belays should be used whenever possible and with modern equipment there are very few occasions when it is not possible to find two satisfactory anchor points. One cannot afford to have a total belay failure in an emergency situation and it is not unknown for an apparently sound belay to fail under load. The belays should be tied in such a way that the strain is evenly distributed and that the failure of one does not increase the amount of slack in the other (Fig. 1). The system should include at least one anchor which will resist the pull in an upward direction which will result from a fall on to a runner. Emphasis should always be given to the correct siting of belays in relation to the direction in which the strain will be imposed should a fall occur. The aim should be to have anchor, belayer and rope in a straight line for if the person belaying is out of line he will receive no direct support from his belay and can easily be pulled off his feet.

The use of nuts when belaying is now a normal and accepted practice and has made it possible to belay safely on stances which have no sound, natural belays provided that the breaking strain of the sling or wire attached to them conforms to the requirements for normal belay slings.

IV. Rope Holding

The rope should be passed around the waist above the belay and controlled by a twist around the wrist of the hand holding the inactive (dead) rope, the climber adopting the stance recommended in the original Tarbuck system. Gloves should be worn at all times. Care should be taken when seconding to pay out smoothly to the leader to ensure that his balance is not upset by a tight rope and the leader should ensure, when bringing up the second, that he keeps the rope just taut, without any slack but not pulling. The action is rather like that of playing a fish, there should be enough pressure to enable one to feel any movement made by the second but not so much that he is receiving any support from the rope.

When belaying in chimneys and other constricted places a shoulder belay may be more convenient. It will also give more traction in the event of the second requiring a pull.

In recent years a number of devices have been developed to attempt to make rope handling and the holding of falling leaders easier and more foolproof. Basically these devices, known collectively as autobelayers, are all friction brakes. The one most commonly in use is the Sticht plate which is the easiest to use and the only one designed specifically for belaying. The figure eight descendeur and Italian hitch can also be used for this purpose (Pl. 5). They can be attached either to the harness of the belayer or directly to an anchor. The latter method is most useful in difficult situations such as stances in etrier where it may be extremely difficult to handle the rope in the normal way. One must have a minimum of two anchor points for the autobelayer in addition to one's own anchors both of which must be absolutely sound and capable of taking an upward pull, for should an anchor fail using this method (which is really only a sophisticated direct belay) there would be no control over the falling climber. When using this system the rope should be fed round the waist in the normal way if at all possible in order to give an additional safeguard against anchor failure.

In most circumstances the preferred method of use is to have the autobelayer attached to the waistbelt so that an indirect belay is given. Using this method it is, with a little practice, quite easy to control a fall but is less useful for bringing up a second, particularly a novice, as it is more difficult to give a tight rope or a pull should this be necessary. It is interesting to note that some novices after using autobelaying devices in drop testing situations and comparing them with waist belays prefer the latter as the strain is better distributed around the body.

One occasionally sees climbers using autobelayers in all situations, but in a normal situation with a good stance and belays they appear to have few real advantages over properly applied conventional techniques when used by experienced climbers. Undoubtedly autobelayers increase the certainty of holding a leader fall, particularly by a novice, and as such have an important part to play in modern rope handling methods. Much of the difficulty experienced when assisting a second can be overcome by practice and experimentation and Sticht plates are now being used regularly by a few mountain centres. It is difficult to say at this stage exactly where they best fit in to the teaching situation and this will be determined to a certain extent by how rock climbing is being taught and to what standard. Their proper place would, at present, appear to lie in the demonstration of advanced techniques and in advanced, multi-pitch rock climbing situations where comparative novices will be safeguarding the leader/instructor.

V. Running Belays, Slings and Karabiners
These should be as strong as circumstances permit. Tape should only be used where it is not possible to use a rope or wire sling for the reasons previously mentioned (see 'Equipment'). When extending a wire sling

with rope or tape the two should always be joined by a karabiner. The sling should *never* be looped directly through the wire as the small radius of the latter creates a knife-edge situation and the sling will break under a very low shock loading. The belief current among many climbers that the plastic sleeve around the wire is to prevent this is quite wrong. The sleeve is in fact put on to reduce the wear on alloy karabiners.

Runner Placing: The leader should aim to get a runner on as quickly as possible after commencing each pitch as this greatly reduces the force of a fall, making the task of the second much easier and increasing the safety of the party in the event of a fall. Ideally a runner should be placed in the first 6–10 ft (1·8–3 m) after leaving the stance *no matter how easy the pitch*, and thereafter at frequent intervals. It is a mistake not to place runners, or to place too few runners, on an easy pitch particularly when instructing. Even on easy ground the unexpected can happen: a loose handhold, a falling stone, even your novice tugging the rope to attract your attention! (It has happened.) Quite apart from these considerations, as an instructor one needs to be constantly aware of the teaching situations and even easy pitches should be utilized to demonstrate runner placings during sessions in which the use of runners is being taught.

VI. Calls
Calls should convey the maximum information as briefly as possible. The following calls are recognized as the acceptable minimum for instructional purposes. When climbing with a regular partner it is possible to simplify them still further. It is important that each call is given at the correct time in the sequence or they can be misleading.

'Taking in' : Called when the leader has reached the stance and is belayed.

'That's me' : Reply from the second as the rope comes tight to his waist.

'Climb when you're ready' : The leader should be holding the rope in the waist belay when he makes this call. On hearing this the second unties his belay (the leader should be expecting this and should take in the extra slack without any further calls being necessary) and calls:

'Climbing' : Before starting the pitch, however, he waits for the final acknowledgement from the leader.

'O.K.'

VII. Extra Calls

Occasionally it is necessary to communicate while actually on a pitch, i.e. one might wish to reverse for a few feet but the leader has the rope in too tightly. The following calls meet most eventualities:

i 'Slack.'
ii 'Take in.'
iii 'Tight.'
iv 'I'm off!'

To work safely and to instil good attitudes towards safety in his students is one of the objectives of any instructor, but what of the other aims which one might hope to achieve during a rock climbing session? These aims should be clearly defined in the mind of the teacher prior to the session, but to arrive at them the following factors need to be taken into consideration:

i Type of course: 'taster' courses; introductory course; advanced course.

Each will demand a different approach. A 'taster' course may be defined as one which introduces the activity without reference to any of the technicalities as opposed to an introductory course as an all-round basic introduction to the sport for those who may wish to progress further.

ii The age and sex of the students.
iii Previous experience.
iv Total time available.
v Number and duration of sessions.
vi Equipment available both personal and communal.
vii Availability of suitable terrain and good teaching situations.
viii Transport requirements.
ix The time of year and likely weather.
x Number of people involved.
xi Number and competence of staff.

All these factors will have a bearing on the final form of the course but the last cannot be too strongly emphasized. In all activities where there is any danger element the expertise and experience of the teacher should be far beyond that required for the proposed work. In many academic subjects it is not unknown for an inexperienced teacher to be only one jump ahead of his pupils but this must not happen in potentially dangerous activities. Should an emergency arise the teacher is going to need a great deal of expertise to deal with it but experience and competence go a long way towards ensuring that emergencies do not arise. Not all hazardous situations are foreseeable but a great many are and the good teacher will, from experience, avoid the potential pitfalls. To teach rock climbing one should have a safe leading standard at least two grades above the level at which one intends to teach.

Teaching Method

Once his aims have been defined the teacher can consider the method in which he hopes to present the subject. In any topic with practical applications the old maxim, 'An ounce of practice is worth a pound of theory', holds good, but some theory must be put across in the case of rock climbing in order to ensure safety on the practical sessions. Much of this can be given at the rock face in fine weather with the advantage of instant clarification of points of terminology and technique.

Many points which one often finds covered in the lecture room are either superfluous or could be dealt with outside. It should always be borne in mind that people attending a rock climbing course, whether absolute beginners having a first taste or advanced students, wish to climb rock not to sit and listen to people talking about it! If we consider the more common of the topics which tend to be introduced to people on rock climbing courses it will be possible to see how best to deal with them.

History of Mountaineering: Certainly not for beginners bursting to have a try at the real thing, it is guaranteed to send them to sleep if introduced first thing after lunch! Very dubious also for the more advanced, but if they show interest in it the instructor should be able to recommend suitable reading.

Ropes: The student on a specialist course should be made aware of the types available, and their comparative size, use, cost and care since he will always wish to know which he should buy. This type of information is normally best given towards the end of a course, probably as an evening session, along with similar information on other items of necessary equipment.

As an introduction the novice really only needs to know that the rope is very strong, that it is easily damaged if stepped upon or otherwise misused and how to tie on to it. (Not even the latter is taught in some 'taster' courses.)

Student teachers are usually told that the average class can only keep its attention concentrated on one thing for about ten minutes and if there is no diversion to refocus the attention of the class within this time it will be lost. The instructor would do well to bear this in mind whatever he happens to be talking about. In the case of rock climbing an obvious natural diversion is knot tying which provides a useful break from the first few minutes on ropes and provides some activity. Every instructor has his own preferred way of teaching a given knot but knowledge of several other methods is useful as it is often found that a student who cannot tie a knot at all by one method finds it easy when shown another. Most mountain centres prefer that all instructors should teach the knot in the same way so that, as in other aspects of the work, conformity is obtained and good continuity of instruction is ensured when the student works with other members of staff. There is nothing more confusing to the novice than to be shown how to do a thing by one instructor and then have this apparently contradicted by another.

Terminology, Theory of Rope Handling, Climbing Calls: These are basic essentials and should be taught on the first session of introductory courses. Given suitable weather they are just as easily taught at the crag as in the lecture room. Time is the enemy of most instructors; they have a lot of information to impart and perhaps only a week in which to do it. In these circumstances the rope handling, etc., is probably best taught directly but given sufficient time the indirect method of posing a problem and allowing the student to discover (with guidance) the answer will pay dividends, e.g. 'Here is a ledge and a large spike of rock, can you tie yourself securely to the spike?' The possibilities of this method are great but it requires time, a safe, controlled situation and an alert instructor.

Protection: The art of protection of the leader has now reached a very high level in this country which is reflected in the rise in standard of the average climber. The novice needs to be aware of the need for runners and the intelligent use of them and, unless one has a good demonstration crag, a blackboard will be found useful for explaining the ways in which runners can be used. We will see in the next section how nuts can be introduced into the practical sessions.

Grading The system of grading is always worth a brief early mention. Novices invariably wish to know the difficulty of what they are attempting and the system can be introduced at this point.

Practical Work

The details set out below are not intended to indicate a hard-and-fast method to be slavishly followed. Rather it is hoped that teachers will tailor their work to suit the needs of their pupils in a way which will make best use of the available facilities. The information given is based on the routine which is followed in many mountain centres.

1. First Session

Terrain: Small outcrops of sound rock, set at an easy angle, with plenty of holds. The top should preferably be flat with good belays and free of loose debris (Pl. 6).

Instruction: Instructor ratios for activities such as rock climbing and other activities with an element of risk have not yet been stipulated by the Department of Education and Science but the following ratios are commonly agreed to be desirable by those fully occupied in this type of work. Instructor/pupil ratios of up to 1:10 are within the limits of safety on small outcrops but 1:4 or 1:5 is much better educationally, enabling much more work to be done in the time available.

'Taster' Sessions: Most people who run these are interested primarily in providing an adventurous situation for the pupils either purely for the sake of the experience or with a view to giving a quick, uncomplicated introduction to the activity. Whatever the reason the accent in this type of course is on maximum practical activity. No attempt is made to teach any ropework and the emphasis is on the child himself solving the problem. The system adopted for maximum efficiency is usually that in which each pupil is given a waistbelt and karabiner, the instructor leads the pitch and brings up each pupil in turn by throwing down an end with a ready tied figure eight knot which only has to be clipped into the karabiner and the gate screwed up. Obviously it is essential when using this technique to choose situations which allow a clear view of the foot of the pitch from the stance in order to ensure that the rope has been clipped in and secured correctly and have a safe area at the top for the children who have been brought up. With two or more instructors working on this system and one working on boulders perhaps setting little problems for those not actually engaged in climbing a maximum of activity can be achieved. For children, who are not particularly interested in learning all about rope handling, etc., but wish to get to grips with the actual climbing, this is a particularly successful approach. Those who find a real interest developing after such a session can be introduced to the finer points at a later date.

Some demonstration and practice of movement on rock could be given on boulders in a 'taster' session and would normally be given in an introductory session. Usually this is based on the principles listed below which are recognized to be the basis of sound rock climbing:

Stand Upright: Best demonstrated on very small holds to show the results of leaning in.

Heels Down: Demonstrate on sloping holds to show how maximum contact between boot sole and rock is obtained.

Hands Low: Relate this to the maintenance of an upright posture.

Three Point Contact: Demonstrate and explain.

Rhythmic Movement: Contrast the effects of jerky and smooth movements when on small holds.

Test Each Hold: Stress that this should become a matter of habit even on often repeated climbs.

Plan Ahead: Explain why and tell them how you would plan a series of moves on that face. Try to let them see how your mind works when climbing.

Small Steps: Show by exaggeration the faults resulting from big steps.

Conserve Energy: Show how novices tend to hold too tightly and use their arms too much.

Think First: This is another way of saying 'Plan ahead' but try to indicate how a little thought can often present an easier solution to the problem.

All demonstrated movements should be emphasized and exaggerated to provide clear illustration. At this stage no rope is necessary on small outcrops of 10 ft (3 m) or so in height with a safe landing and the student can be allowed to practise the above points with *constructive* criticism from the instructor. It is, for example, useless to say 'That's no good' with no explanation. He needs to know why it is no good and how he can improve it. Often the novice will not be able to understand what he is doing wrong unless you get up there and exaggerate his fault for him to see.

The instructor needs to have a sharp eye in order to detect faults as they occur and in addition to this he must be capable of analysing a movement so that he is able to pinpoint the reason for an incorrect execution of it and explain this to the student. He further needs to be a good mimic in order to demonstrate a fault and its correction in the clearest possible manner.

Introductory Sessions

When the group has begun to get the feel of the rock it can be introduced to the various types of handhold and foothold and the major techniques, mantelshelfing, jamming, chimneying and laybacking, if facilities for practice of these are available. If time is short it may be preferred to leave these until the second session so that some ropework may be covered. Much will depend on the size of the group but plenty of free movement at this stage will quickly familiarize the student with his new environment and the techniques necessary to master it. He will, at the same time, be gaining confidence in his boots and his ability to stand on what are to him small holds. During this initial stage students can be given a selection of nuts and allowed to place them in what they consider to be suitable locations around the base of the cliff. In this way they soon become familiar with the basic techniques of nut insertion and will begin to develop an eye for likely placings.

The introduction to ropework should be given on short, easy climbs where success is assured, preferably the ones which have just been soloed. Thus fear, which greatly inhibits the learning process, is eliminated and the student can concentrate on the ropework and the calling system. Each student should have the opportunity of bringing someone up but with the instructor at his side to offer advice and to be in a position to control the rope immediately if necessary. This should only be done in safe situations where the confidence of the second will not be affected by having an inexperienced person holding the rope and is best not done at all with children until they have had considerable rock climbing experience. Clear, correct calling, even when only a few feet apart, is essential if a sound basis for future work is to be built up. The instructor should keep a sharp eye open for handling faults, in particular too much slack, letting go of the rope to point out holds, etc., and leaning forward to give directions. Belaying faults are many but at this stage one should mainly be concerned with the basics: has the student succeeded in securing himself to the cliff, are his knots correct, are his belays taut and has he placed himself in the correct position to be supported by the belay in relation to the direction in which the pull is expected to be?

After a few climbs, practice in holding a falling second may be introduced, the victim being the instructor who should be able to simulate the situation with no danger to himself. This can be done in three stages.

i Let the student hold the dead-weight to gain an impression of the weight involved.

ii Fall with warning while actually moving.

iii Fall without warning other than that you are likely to come off somewhere en route.

Abseiling
This can be introduced into the first session or may be given a whole session to itself if time allows. Most students get a lot of fun out of it when they have overcome the initial fear of leaning backwards and then often want to have several tries. This is not usually possible if abseiling has been combined with the first session unless the staff/pupil ratio is a good one.

When teaching abseiling the following points are important.

i A safety rope should always be used.

ii Separate belays for the abseil and safety ropes should be used and the reason explained.

iii The instructor should have the student in view all the way down.

iv First abseils should be short, about 30 ft (9 m) is sufficient.

v A slab with a rounded top gives the easiest start for an abseil.

vi An abseil rope which is belayed well above the start ledge is to be preferred. Belays which are at foot level when setting off are difficult to start from, unnerving for the novice and should be avoided.

vii A little time explaining the dangers of jump abseils is well spent. It is a sobering thought that abseiling, considered by most climbers to be easy, accounts for a considerable number of serious accidents.

viii Helmets should be worn at all times. Gloves are optional, opinions differ on this point but on short abseils should not be necessary except, of course, for the person managing the safety rope.

Young children often find great difficulty in abseiling using the conventional karabiner abseil as their shoulder width is insufficient to prevent the rope slipping off. In these circumstances the use of a figure eight descendeur is a better alternative and is easily managed by young children. Due to their low body-weight it is usually much easier for them to descend on a single rope rather than double when using this method.

2. Second Session

Terrain: Small cliffs giving climbs of more than one pitch with good stances and belays. The cliffs should preferably present a wide variety of situations: chimney, crack, slab, wall, etc., and a reasonable range of difficulty. Climbs with intermediate stances large enough to accommodate the whole party are ideal from a teaching point of view.

Instruction: Ratios should be a maximum of 1:4 but 1:2 is desirable for really good teaching. On multi-pitch climbs everything becomes very cumbersome and slow if numbers are high and there is inevitably a great deal of time wasted by people hanging around unless alternative activities are introduced for those waiting their turn.

During the earlier sessions the student will have been introduced to an unfamiliar element and will have been able to practise a variety of basic techniques. He should now be feeling more at home in his surroundings, more confident and looking forward to doing some 'real' climbs.

The aim of this session should be to consolidate what has been learned so far and also to take the student a stage further in his development as a rock climber. If good terrain has been chosen he will be able to do two pitch climbs where it becomes necessary to adopt the correct change-over sequence in belaying and he will also begin to be aware of the height factor as the climbs should be longer than those of the first session. More emphasis on the use of running belays can be made in this session. He has already experimented with nut placings, perhaps had a little theory on the use of runners and has possibly seen them used during the first session. Now his attention can be really drawn to them and their purpose as they are used.

Very few crags have all the features to which one would like to introduce beginners and one is fortunate indeed if one has such a crag available for training purposes. Often, features which are lacking on a crag may be found among the boulders at the foot. Hand-jamming cracks in boulders are usually better than ones in cliffs because the students are able to observe exactly what takes place in the crack by observing from above and the instructor in turn can observe easily when the technique is being practised (Pl. 7). Mantelshelf problems and laybacks can also be found on boulders and put to good use but care should be taken to ensure that the examples chosen are not too hard for the students. Success breeds success and such things as arm's length mantelshelves and overhanging laybacks tend to be discouraging when one has not got the technique to cope with them!

A drawback with many otherwise suitable cliffs is that the belays on the top are poor or non-existent. This can be remedied by placing pegs or even by cementing in permanent ones if the crag is little used by ordinary climbers and is infinitely preferable to using poor belays.

As the session progresses students often express a desire to do something hard, they wish to try out their newfound skills to the limit of their ability. If the crag has a suitable range the standard can be raised gradually to give them a taste of difficulty but it must be emphasized that students who are not finding things too easy, particularly nervous students, should on no account be allowed to attempt climbs on which they stand no chance of succeeding. This is bad instruction and there is no more certain way of destroying what little confidence a student may have gained. Some crags have an abundance of boulder problems in the vicinity and these can often be used to advantage towards the end of a session to introduce the more eager to difficulty while the less able can still do easier problems on the same boulder. It will often be found that boulder problems do a great deal to increase confidence as students can go to their absolute limit on very small handholds and footholds in complete safety and gain a lot of valuable experience in discovering just what will support them on a rock face.

It is a mistake, when instructing a group of mixed ability, to leave the less able sitting around while the others are taking up something more difficult. The level of instruction should be such that all can participate and benefit. A well co-ordinated team of instructors should be able to make a rough assessment of ability during the first session and arrange the students into ability groups for future sessions.

The above outline would form the basis of a minimum introduction to rock climbing either as an experience, through the medium of a 'taster' course, or with a view to carrying on with the activity. Progression from this point, time permitting, would be via a series of sessions to consolidate the initial work, preferably on a variety of cliffs and presenting a range of techniques and situations, on climbs of a fairly low standard of difficulty. Given a school situation where there can be a continuity of instruction over a long period progression can continue to an advanced level in a gradual and controlled way as the teacher will have a very sound knowledge of his students, their abilities and weaknesses. In the centre situation, however, the majority of the work will usually be at a basic level with beginners. Of these some may continue climbing through a club or with friends, others may return to take an advanced course if it is available. In the next chapter we shall examine the aspects and implications of advanced instruction.

Chapter Two

Progressions in Rock Climbing

Within the teaching context advanced rock climbing does not necessarily mean hard rock climbing. The students have not come to be guided up hard routes but to improve their knowledge of the sport and to go away better equipped to pursue it at their own level with friends. A taste of harder climbing has its place within a scheme of advanced training but is by no means the only objective. The first essential, even if all the students are known to you, is a revision session to find out what they have retained of the rope handling and to correct any faults. The instructor will also have the chance to make an estimate of the range of ability within the group and should be in a position by the end of the session to decide which routes are going to be most suited to the immediate needs of each individual.

The complete revision, including plenty of practice will probably occupy the first day and then, if all is satisfactory, the group can be introduced to big cliffs with reasonably easy climbs of 200 ft (61 m) or more without exposure. As in all training on multi-pitch climbs the best routes are those on which the whole party can be assembled at each stance before the leader moves off again. This ensures that the instructor is able to see each person climbing and is able to keep control of the rope handling. He is also able to ensure that each person is correctly belayed and discuss the problems of the next pitch with the whole group. In order to be able to choose good teaching routes the instructor must have a good knowledge of his area and be familiar with all the climbs best suited to his needs. At this stage it is unwise for an instructor to embark upon a route about which he knows nothing. Many routes which are apparently quite easy are totally unsuitable for beginners, the classic Welsh example being Spiral Stairs on Dinas Cromlech in the Llanberis Pass. The guide-book grading is only 'Hard Difficult' and in fact the actual climbing is quite easy but the route starts from the foot of Cenotaph Corner well up the cliff with a 70-ft (21 m) traverse above an overhang. The leader cannot see the second, communication is difficult, the rock is not above suspicion and the difficult move is the first one! Places such as this are best avoided unless one knows the party well.

For all work on big cliffs the instructor/student ratio should be 1:2 which makes advanced instruction an expensive proposition in terms of staff required. However, it cannot be too strongly emphasized that this ratio is absolutely necessary both from safety and teaching angles. Climbs with stances where it is possible to gather a party of more than three are few and far between which means that the instructor has no contact with anyone on his rope other than the second and, possibly, third man. He is unable to see them climbing and can therefore offer no advice and has no control over the rope handling or belaying. The author has witnessed the extreme case of a party on Flying Buttress, a popular teaching route and the longest on Dinas Cromlech, where the leader had reached the top of the cliff before the last man had left the ground!

If the programme is reasonably flexible it can be varied to suit the weather but sometime, preferably early in the course, some drop testing should be introduced. The one thing which the average climber lacks most is practice in holding a falling leader. This can easily be simulated without sophisticated equipment but with most of the simpler devices much labour is expended in raising the weight. With ingenuity a rig such as that designed and built by Roger Orgil, the deputy director at Plas y Brenin, can be made at quite a low cost and will take much of the labour out of the lifting (Pl. 8). The weight should be about that of a light leader and the holder should be well padded around the waist where the rope runs. It goes without saying that gloves need to be worn and the rope should be an old one kept especially for the purpose. Great care needs to be taken when using drop testing devices to give practice in holding free falls as the strains involved are considerable and there have been several instances of people receiving leg and back injuries when not standing correctly. Progression from holding the weight without any fall to holding it from a drop of a few feet should be gradual. Most modern climbing situations involve the use of running belays and it is therefore preferable to concentrate most of the drop test work on the situation which is more likely to be experienced in practice, namely a fall held through runners rather than to overstress the free falling situation with its attendant dangers when practised. The use of a drop-tester will quickly make the student aware of the forces involved in holding a falling leader and how drastically these are reduced by the use of runners. It will further make him conscious of the importance of his stance relative to the line of fall and the vital necessity of sound belays. It is always interesting to watch the way in which people ensure that belays are absolutely taut and stances correct when they *know* that they are going to have to hold a fall. If the instructor can get his students to view all belaying situations in this light he is doing them a great service.

This work with a group of ten will easily consume a half-day session but needs to be combined with some other aspect of the work, perhaps prusiking or aid climbing, if students are to be kept fully occupied. The other half-day can well be spent by going back to short climbs and concentrating on hard, single pitch problems. The value of these in advanced work is high. The students are encouraged to develop their technique by being put into situations where they have to do certain things to succeed which they have been able to avoid on easier climbs such as standing on a really small hold or trusting to a hand jam. Their behaviour under stress can be noted, and valuable insight gained into their capability to cope with bigger and more serious routes. Technical skill will be evident but the instructor should be on the look-out for the less obvious things: 'push', perhaps best defined as the determination to succeed, and physical strength, fitness and agility. Many students tire easily if they lead sedentary occupations and this sort of information will be important when it comes to deciding the programme for the latter part of the training.

A good idea at this stage is to rig up a pulley belay system on a climb which the students have not done before and they can then work out the solution for themselves, protecting each other from the ground in a position from which they are able to observe what is happening and give advice to each other. This is particularly useful with really able students who want to get their teeth into something as it can be set up to give complete control over something short and hard where the solution is not obvious. The role of the instructor at this stage is as observer, checking the safety angles and keeping careful note of how the problem is met. After the climb has been completed the way in which it was done can be discussed and alternative solutions pointed out or demonstrated. This helps to develop the ability to size up a pitch before attempting it.

Progression should now be to long, fairly easy climbs with some exposure and with an increase in difficulty as the student gains in confidence and ability. The use of runners should now be common-place on all climbs and the student should be completely familiar with them. Wherever possible each pitch should be discussed with the party before it is done. As with the short climbs try to get them into the habit of assessing the pitch, how it is best tackled, the location of obvious runner or nut placings and likely resting places. In this way they will come to rely on their judgement rather than a word-for-word description from the guide-book. They should come to see the guide in its true perspective, an indication of whether the climb is worth while with enough information on pitches to enable the climber to find his way while exercising skill and judgement in doing so.

A technique which is insufficiently practised by most British climbers is that of reversing and some should be included in advanced training. Apart from the actual practice in reversing there is a secondary benefit to be gained. As the student climbs down he can place runners to safeguard the descent of the last man and thus get used to the feel of putting on runners and finding suitable placings while safeguarded by a rope from above. This is good exercise for training leaders and will be dealt with more fully in the next section.

Training Leaders

On completion of a one-week advanced course of training the average student should be competent to second climbs up to 'Hard Very Difficult' or 'Severe' in standard and should have done a variety of climbs involving all the major techniques. We would also expect him to have done some basic rescue work during the course and to have received background information on the choice and care of equipment, climbing areas, the use of guide-books and simple map reading. He should also know the location of the climbing clubs in his home area and the relevant addresses of secretaries, etc. His ropework should be sound and, in a nutshell, he ought to be a competent second. However it is extremely likely that he wishes to lead and if he goes away without having had any instruction in leading or any chance to lead in a controlled situation it may be thought that the training organization has failed in this vital respect.

Many people say that good leaders are born, not made, and while this may be true to a certain extent it is also fair to say that all leaders, even 'natural' ones, have to make a start and there are many ways in which that start can be made more easily and safely. Leader training is seldom attempted at mountain centres for a variety of sound reasons, the most important being that centres have to maintain high standards of safety and the accident risk is higher in leader training. People seldom go to a centre for a sufficiently long period of time for the staff to form any detailed estimate of their capabilities and unless one is really sure of the student's technical ability, emotional make-up and possible reaction to potentially dangerous situations it is unwise to let him lead. Needless to say it is not possible to form such an estimate from the knowledge obtained of a student in one week. However, if students are going to receive regular instruction over a period of time, i.e. at school, college or youth club and wish to progress to leading (as they inevitably will) one should not evade the issue and hope that they will learn this all-important aspect of the sport by themselves. Many people shirk their responsibilities in this direction simply because they feel that they cannot control the situation but the problem exists and it has to be faced squarely.

No instructor wishes to be involved in a situation where a student is exposed to risks which are beyond his control but this situation does exist even on the easiest of leads. The instructor can never be absolutely certain that the student will not fall off but it is my firm belief that if the problem is approached in the right way the chances of accident are extremely low. The student leader should in fact be safer than the average leader attempting a climb which he has not done before. He will, if trained correctly, have undergone a logical progression from seconding to leading and he will have the benefit of his instructor's knowledge and experience. His early leads will be hand-picked to suit his requirements. Obviously the calibre of instructor for leader training should be very high. One would expect this to be the province of the holder of the M.I.A.C. or of an instructor whose rock climbing ability is known to be well up to this standard. The possession of M.I.C. although adequate for most situations is not sufficient in this case. In addition the instructor needs to be totally familiar with the training climbs which he intends to use. Even the best of instructors cannot be expected to give of his best in an unfamiliar area and should certainly not attempt to teach leading in such a situation.

The following stages of training are intended as a broad outline and within this framework much variation is possible. The training will always have to be adjusted to the capabilities, physique and temperament of the individual.

Good Rope Management is the first essential. Until the student is thoroughly competent in all aspects and can be relied upon to belay correctly without supervision he is not ready to lead no matter how high his technical expertise.

High Technical Proficiency as a second is necessary to ensure reasonable safety when leading easy climbs. A seconding standard of 'Severe' should be expected before a student is introduced to 'Moderate' and 'Difficult' leads.

Familiarity to Exposure will help to increase confidence when leading easy climbs.

Descending Climbs, as previously mentioned, trains the student to reverse moves which he has made and it helps him to consider a move in terms of 'Can I make it?' and 'Can I reverse it if I cannot make the next one?' Placing runners will not only give practice but will also put the student in the position of having to decide on the best placings to protect a leader and lead him to consider the problems of drag and situations where a runner may be placed to protect one member of the party or other situations where it may be omitted for the same reasons, i.e. on a pitch which has a difficult traverse followed by a vertical section the leader may decide not to place runners on the traverse in order to give the second a more direct rope.

Traverses done as last man are a good intermediate stage between seconding and leading. A good instructor will be able to grade these so that at first the harder moves come towards the end of the traverse where there is little rope out, then later at the beginning.

Aid Climbing could be introduced at this stage, or even earlier as it gives experience of steep rock and a great deal of practice in handling equipment and ropes in awkward situations. Clipping ropes into runners, a thing with which many inexperienced leaders have difficulty, begins to become second nature after a few sessions of aid climbing.

The First True Leads are best made on one-pitch climbs which have first been seconded and then descended placing runners. They should be easy and well protected. If this method is adopted the safety and success factors are kept as high as possible. For a first lead it is advisable to leave the runners in place if the route has been descended, or if not they should be placed by the instructor beforehand, so that the student can concentrate entirely on the climbing and just clip into each runner as it comes within his reach. The number of occasions on which the instructor will need to do this will vary according to the ability of the individual. After a few routes it should only be necessary for the instructor to place the occasional good runner leaving the student to locate and find the majority.

Selected Pitches on longer climbs which are easy and have previously been seconded can now be led.

Longer Climbs previously seconded can be led in their entirety or student leaders can be paired to lead through on their own with the instructor keeping an eye on the proceedings. Students usually get a great deal of pleasure and satisfaction from this work in pairs and it greatly increases leading confidence.

One-Pitch Climbs which have not previously been seconded should now be well within the capabilities of the student. They should be carefully chosen and the difficulties likely to be met, the techniques used and the places where protection can be arranged should be discussed and pointed out prior to commencement. On all applicable stages the student should be using the guide-book to locate the climbs. Because the instructor knows the area so well it is automatic to walk up to the foot of the climb without giving it a thought but it is of much more value to allow the student to work this out for himself.

On completion of this stage the student should be well on the way to becoming a competent leader and the instructor's job from henceforth will be to direct him to climbs which are correctly graded and within his capabilities while he gains leading experience and occasionally to take him up harder climbs to encourage him to spread his wings a little. As he seconds the harder routes he will now view them with the eye of a leader.

At all stages when choosing routes the instructor must be prepared to take into account the protection available, particularly at the crux, the state of the weather and the condition of the rock and weigh these against the known abilities of his student. At no time should a student be 'pushed' or hurried and it should be strongly emphasized from the outset that he must descend if at all doubtful of his ability to make a move safely, rather than press on and risk a fall. Continual emphasis should be laid upon the importance of adequate protection and smooth, deliberate, carefully thought-out movements.

Training leaders puts an enormous amount of responsibility on to the shoulders of those brave enough to accept it and with sufficient awareness to realize that they cannot morally avoid it if they have taken beginners to this stage. It does, however, have its rewards. One of the truly satisfying moments of an instructing career is to be taken up a really hard climb by an ex-pupil and know that one's labours have borne fruit.

Aid Climbing

Aid climbing is an integral part of modern rock climbing and ought to at least be introduced during advanced instruction. As with most other practical subjects, the sooner the student gets out and does it the better, but a little theory on the equipment required and in particular the modern developments in peg design and material can be of value. The simple theory of the technique is also useful but this can be demonstrated in practice far more easily than in theory and is best done outside.

Practical Work

Terrain: For an introduction a short cliff with the pegs permanently in place is ideal. It should not be overhanging but needs to be almost vertical. If the angle of the face is too easy the beginner usually encounters difficulty in getting his feet into the etrier. As ideal rock faces are difficult to find some instructors tend to make use of trees, which can be found at any angle and the pegs can be placed exactly where desired. On the debit side some difficulty is usually encountered due to the roundness of the trunk, the student tends to slip round in situations where he would easily have been able to brace on a cliff. Beech trees lend themselves to this work as they take pegs very well. If trees are going to be used they should be in a situation where the pegs can be left in permanently as they are hard to remove and this would result in damage to the tree.

Instruction: 1:6 is the ideal ratio but up to 1:10 is quite manageable.
The equipment to be used should be examined and its use explained.

In general etrier are easier for a novice to use than tapes but if the American single-rope method is being taught with leg crossing for stability tapes are necessary. The placing and removal of pegs in horizontal and vertical cracks can be demonstrated and practised if it is intended to give more than an introduction to the activity; also the methods of determining the firmness of pegs and how to decrease the leverage if the peg is too long. For a 'taster' course only a demonstration of the technique on fixed pegs needs to be given and provided that the pegs are known to be absolutely firm there is no reason why the students should not be allowed to lead their own little climbs. Due to the time factor it will be found that these practice climbs are best limited to four or five pegs and an instructor can usually keep an eye on two such climbs at once provided that they are close together. In doing their own leading on such climbs with sound, well-placed pegs the students get a quick insight into the complexity of the ropework in complete safety. Many will feel strange to be on the front end of the rope but they do not equate this with normal leading as distances are short and the pegs give a feeling of security.

From here, if aid climbing is to be pursued beyond an introduction, short climbs on which the student has to place or, if climbing as a second, remove the pegs form the next stage. This is followed by proper aid pitches led by the instructor and later, possibly as an aid to leader training, students working in pairs as leader and second on A1 pitches of around 30 ft (9 m) in height with good peg cracks. The instructor should be familiar with the climbs and be able to advise on peg requirements, etc. The climbs should finish on a good top with good belays which is easily accessible to the instructor. A further link between aid climbing and training for free climbing is that the student quickly develops the skills of sound peg placing for belays, particularly if those not engaged in holding ropes are allowed to experiment with peg placings around the foot of the cliff.

Prusiking

Prusiking is a minor but very important skill which is often overlooked. The general attitude is that it is simple and would be easy to do should the occasion arise. A little practice soon puts matters into perspective. Have *you* ever tried to fix prusiks while hanging free from the end of a rope? If you have not, try it but be sure that you can get your feet on the ground if you fail! It is best to practise this in company for reasons of safety.

The introduction to prusiking can be done in conjunction with an artificial session or a session of drop testing and in this way a group can be kept occupied the whole time. A rope over a tree branch arranged so that the student can have his feet against the trunk to prevent spinning is good for a beginning and for an introduction it is best that prusiking is commenced from standing on the ground. Once the skill of moving up the rope has been practised a realistic situation can be introduced by arranging the rope so that it hangs free and that students cannot touch the ground when tied on the end. The rope should be secured in such a way that it can be easily and quickly released when a student is attached for all prusiking sessions as people often fail to get their weight off the rope at the first realistic attempt and can quickly become sick and dizzy due to the constriction of breathing and spinning. Ordinary Prusik knots, Bachman knots, Klemheist knots and the various mechanical devices all have their places and all should be shown and tried. If time is restricted, however, it is best to demonstrate the non-mechanical methods only. They are undoubtedly efficient if practised and can be a lifesaver when other, more specialized equipment is not carried.

Prusiking, once learned, can fill several hours of a bad day to advantage. Prusiking championships and the like can be arranged on a time basis. The time being taken from the moment the competitor swings free until he touches the attachment of the rope. This type of pastime gives a lot of amusement and much useful knowledge of prusiking situations is gained indirectly in this way. All work of this type should be strictly supervised as many people are likely to throw caution to the winds when a competitive element is introduced.

There are many variations on the basic method of prusiking but one of the most popular, particularly in situations where long sections of prusiking have to be done, is that which employs a full sit-sling or Whillans type harness and a kicking sling. This method is also a good one for teaching as at any stage in the proceedings the student can rest for as long as necessary in the sit-sling and sort things out. Basically the method works as follows: a sling is attached to the rope with a prusik-type knot or device and is clipped into the sit-sling so that it can be pushed to arm's length when standing upright. *Below* this a short sling is attached with a second prusiker. One foot is placed in the short (kicking) sling and one then stands upright, pulling on the rope with the hands, slides up the upper prusiker to its full extent and immediately sits in the sit-sling (Pl. 9 a, b, c). From this resting position the kicking sling is slid up as high as possible and the process is repeated. The more gymnastic will find that by leaning backwards the leg, and consequently the kicking sling, can be lifted higher. It should be pointed out to students that the length of prusiking slings is an individual matter and that everyone going into a situation where it may be necessary to prusik in an emergency should know the length of sling best suited to them and, in some circumstances, e.g. badly crevassed wet glacier, have them already attached to the rope.

Choice and Care of Equipment

The job of a climbing instructor or teacher with responsibility for out-door activities in a school embraces considerably more than the actual instructing. He will be responsible for the maintenance of the equip-ment in his care, he may be appointed to maintain the whole of the centre climbing equipment and it may be his duty to buy and replace equipment from year to year. Thus any instructor should know the essentials of choosing the correct equipment for the needs of his organization, maintaining it in good order and detecting wear and damage. The following points may be of help in this respect.

Ropes: Ropes for rock climbing must be No. 4 laid nylon or 11 mm kernmantel. A certain amount of preference goes into the choice but it is worth noting that a kernmantel rope suffers major damage more easily than a laid rope due to the fact that the outer sheath contributes quite considerably to the total strength. Thus if this sheath is ruptured the rope has to be discarded. When examining the ropes for wear and tear it is also more difficult to spot major damage as one cannot see the state of the core which can, in some circumstances, be badly torn or severed without obvious damage to the outer sheath. It is also more expensive than laid rope which may be an important consideration when working to a budget. Laid ropes should be to BS 3104 and kernmantel should meet the requirements of the U.I.A.A. specification for ropes. Kern-mantel is pleasanter to handle and less subject to kinking than laid rope and when advanced work is being done it is useful to be able to show, use and compare both types of rope, but if the work is largely basic then laid rope alone is adequate.

The average length of rope used for instructional purposes is 120–

150 ft (36–45 m) but in many circumstances this is far too long. It is preferable with beginners to have lengths suited to the cliff which is normally used for training. This has several advantages, the first being that there is not a great deal of slack lying around to be trodden on by clumsy feet, the second is that beginners find shorter ropes easier to handle, and the third that the outlay on ropes is less. On the other hand in areas where belays are poor and on advanced work it may be necessary to have 150-ft (45 m) ropes.

Always keep spare ropes in stock so that a rope damaged in use may be replaced immediately. Frequent, careful checks should be made on the condition of the ropes and in particular an eye should be kept open for cuts and serious areas of abrasion. When in doubt downgrade the rope. A worn laid rope is indicated by a flattening of the lay (Pl. 10) and it may also have a lifeless feel. General wear in kernmantel ropes is harder to detect but any damage to the sheath, other than minor abrasion, is serious and lumpiness or varying diameter may be an indication of damage to the core.

Although no definite conclusions have yet been reached regarding the safe life of a rope it is generally agreed that ropes being used regularly for instruction on serious (multi-pitch) climbs should be replaced each year. The National Engineering Laboratory is carrying out tests on climbing ropes and, although no final conclusions have been reached, latest results indicate that the safe life is at least a hundred climbing days for both laid and kernmantel ropes. The old ropes still have plenty of life in them and may be used with safety for short climbs and basic work for one or more years according to the type of work and the amount of wear. Discarded ropes have a variety of uses but there should be no chance of them being used again for climbing. It is therefore advisable to adopt a colour coding scheme so that ropes can easily be identified. The whole rope may be dyed or, more simply, the ends can be painted. In addition a written record of the ropes and slings should be kept so that it is possible to check on exactly how long a rope or set of slings has been in use.

Ropes should be well coiled when stored and it is the responsibility of all users to see that they are returned to the store in good order. A little time spent in coiling at the end of a session is to be preferred to a store full of kinked and untidy ropes. Everybody likes to take a nicely coiled rope out but there is a tendency, particularly when the weather is bad, not to return them that way. The usual excuse is that the novices have been coiling them for practice. Fine, and this should be so, but if their efforts are not successful then at the end of the day the instructor should put them to rights. Any fault noticed while a rope is in use should be reported to the person in charge of the equipment and the rope should be marked in some way for ease of identification.

Ropes are best stored in a cool, airy room away from direct light and should be hung for the air to circulate round them. If they become muddy and gritty during a bad day it pays to wash them thoroughly in a stream at the end of the session. The abrasive qualities of grit can cause rapid deterioration in a climbing rope once it works its way into the lay.

Slings: The most economic way to equip with slings is to purchase a length of rope of the required diameter and cut it to the sizes required. Laid slings should have their ends whipped and then fused but with kernmantel and tape, fusing is sufficient. The knots used to join the slings should be checked on each outing and tightened if necessary. The double fisherman's knot is the accepted knot for rope slings and the tape knot for tape. Slings receive considerable wear and usually need replacing more frequently than ropes. They should be checked often and must never be made from old ropes. Tape is highly dangerous if it receives even the tiniest nick on the edge and should be discarded.

Harnesses: Harnesses are now accepted by most centres as they are better able to spread a load than waistlines and direct ties. They are usually easier to fit than waistlines and not subject to such rapid deterioration. The most popular types for use by children are the Irvine/Moac belt and the Troll belt. Both are simple, broad belts which fit around the waist. The former has a metal, two-part buckle which is locked by the karabiner which attaches the rope to the belt and the latter has a plain buckle which is designed to be double threaded. Both have their advantages and disadvantages. The Irvine is safely and simply locked once the karabiner is in place but should a pupil fall off or have a tight rope the buckle can dig into his ribs causing discomfort and bruising. Care needs to be taken with the Troll belt to ensure that students do not forget to double thread the buckle as the belt will open easily under a light load if only single threaded. Otherwise the belt is cheap, comfortable and the buckle does not tend to dig in to the same extent as that of the Irvine. The way in which harnesses fasten should really be a minor point, provided that the end-result is sound, as any good instructor will be in the habit of checking all his pupils each time they tie on to see that all is correct and secure.

Karabiners: There is now a U.I.A.A. standard for karabiners and all those meeting the requirements of this (which stipulate minimum breaking strains permissible along the short axis as well as the long) carry the U.I.A.A. stamp of approval (Pl. 11). For belaying and attaching the climbing rope to the waist harness only steel screwgate karabiners conforming to the above standard should be used. The hinge and pin of any karabiner should be oiled frequently, also the screwgates where applicable. After a wet day it is advisable to dry the karabiners and rub them over with an oily rag. Karabiners which are used regularly on sea-cliffs should be washed in warm, fresh water after use and oiled, irrespective of whether they have been in the water or not. Salt spray can be just as damaging as immersion if not dealt with. Check occasionally for wear, particularly at the hinge where excessive side play may be felt. It is always best to buy karabiners over the counter if possible as many tend to have side-play and other defects, such as badly fitting gates or weak springs when new, due to poor quality control.

Helmets: Helmets are now an accepted part of the climbers' equipment and any helmet is certainly better than none but a good one is to be preferred. There is now a British Standard for climbing helmets and there is, at the moment, at least one helmet on the market which meets the requirement. Helmets should be capable of absorbing the shock resulting from impact and this is ideally done with a crushable liner but after one hard knock the helmet is useless. Almost as good is a foam liner which absorbs shock but regains its resilience afterwards and is able to take further loading. Most manufacturers tend to use the latter with a fibreglass or plastic outer shell. Some helmets may be obtained with adjustable headbands to suit several head sizes. These are obviously very useful to those who need to keep a stock of helmets to issue to a range of people on courses.

Boots: Boots are an expensive item, rock climbing and high mountain boots particularly so, and students should be made aware of the need to keep them clean and well polished to help protect them against the effects of soaking in acid waters of mountain and moorland. 'Drypacks' containing silica gel, used in the boots while in the store will dry them out gently and completely. The dangers of drying boots rapidly by putting them in drying rooms or close to fires and radiators should be pointed out. The best treatment for the leather is ordinary boot polish with an occasional coat of 'Wet-Prufe'. Centre boots for hire to students have to be multi-purpose and are not usually good enough for hard climbing. People attending specialist courses should be encouraged to get their own if possible. If students arrive with their own boots they should be checked for suitability and condition.

Anoraks: If fully waterproof, plastic-impregnated anoraks are normally used, which is the case at many centres, a set of cheap, strong cloth anoraks should also be provided for rock climbing as ropework and abseiling will quickly strip the plastic coating and spoil the anorak. It is also inadvisable to use plastic-surfaced suits in true winter conditions as the low frictional properties make the suit into a lethal toboggan should the wearer slip. Even on gentle slopes novices find it hard to control slides in these garments and a better alternative in these conditions is a proofed nylon suit which does not have such a smooth outer surface.

Organization

A climbing day requires good organization if all is to go smoothly and safely. The points given below are all important and the person in charge of the activity should habitually work to a system along these lines.

Before leaving the centre check that there are sufficient ropes, karabiners and slings for the session and that all the party have helmets and gloves. Packed lunches should also be checked if the party is going to be out for the day.

Check that transport is laid on if required and, if the vehicle is not staying out, ensure that the time and place of pick-up for the return journey is understood.

Team the students by ability if possible and allocate them to instructors. As a general rule the weaker students should be allocated to the more experienced instructors in order to get the best out of them. Young, inexperienced instructors, often with high technical ability, tend to lack the insight into the problems of beginners which is necessary to deal with those who have little aptitude or who are nervous. Therefore they are better suited in the main to the more competent students. This is not always the case and so the instructor in charge needs to know both staff and students well if he is to make the best use of their abilities.

Check which climbs are proposed and if necessary make other recommendations to over-ambitious instructors who may not know the area so well as yourself. Make sure that all instructors are familiar with the cliff. If not, devote some time to ensuring that they choose suitable climbs for their groups and that they can find the starts and know the descriptions. Let the others know where you will be climbing should any emergency arise and where a comprehensive first aid kit is to be found. Lastly arrange a definite time and place to regroup.

General Instructional Points

Many of these points are obvious, commonsense things, yet often they are overlooked.

Always check knots at the start of a climb and again during the ascent. Make the check obvious to beginners, it increases their confidence in your ability to look after them. Do not fail to check the competent also but try not to make it obvious, a glance will suffice if you know what you are looking for.

Choose demonstration places which are as near perfect as possible and make your demonstrations as smooth and as controlled as you can.

When engaged on climbs of more than one pitch try to choose them so that you can get all your students up to each stance before continuing.

Avoid traverses with beginners.

If you are making use of voluntary or temporary help check that they know the area and if not give them the benefit of your knowledge regarding suitable climbs, ways off, etc. Always find out which routes they intend to do. Most voluntary instructors come to a centre with a genuine desire to help plus the hope that they are going to get some personal climbing in. There is a tendency, which has to be guarded against, for them to do climbs which are keen to do as opposed to those which are best suited to the needs of the students. Make sure that all voluntary instructors are familiar with your method of rope handling and that they use it themselves when instructing.

It is dangerous to allow students to practise unroped on outcrops above drops or boulder fields.

Choose routes which are well within your capabilities when instructing and do not hesitate to come down if you come up against something which you feel is risky under the prevailing conditions. An instructor should be aware of the fact that he cannot rely on a novice to hold his rope in the event of a fall and should therefore treat the route as though he were soloing. Even on routes which are easy, well known and oft repeated, instructors should always put on plenty of runners both as an example to the novice and to increase their own chances of being held should a fall occur.

When working with trainee leaders it is often advantageous to solo so that one can move about from party to party keeping an eye on rope-work, belaying, etc., and also to rig a pitch with runners if necessary. There are obvious dangers to this, even on very easy rock, and these cannot be entirely eliminated. They can however be reduced in the following ways.

i Put fixed ropes down the routes which you are likely to use the most.

ii Wear a harness and prusiking device to clip into the fixed ropes wherever possible so that you can protect yourself as you climb.

iii In the absence of a fixed rope clip into the climbing rope when the leader is belayed and climb the pitch before the second starts to climb.

iv Do not stand about unbelayed on stances, clip into the belay system with a sling or your prusiker.

v Do not solo immediately behind another climber or in a situation where the climbing rope could sweep you off should another climber fall.

vi Some Jumar castings have been known to fail under load and as this is otherwise a highly satisfactory prusiking device it is now common practice to link the strong points with tape to distribute the load and increase the points of attachment to guard against failure of one section. One method of doing this is shown in Pl. 12.

vii Stay alert to the dangers of your situation. It is very easy when soloing and instructing to become engrossed in the latter and forget that one is solo.

Avoid climbs which you have not done before and about which you have no reliable information. Many of the easier climbs are not suited to beginners for one reason or another.

Students tend to take off crash helmets at the top of a climb, particularly on hot days. Explain the dangers of this and see that they keep them on until they are back down at the foot of the cliff and completely out of range of falling stones.

Whenever possible arrange your belays so that you have a clear view of the pitch. You cannot give sound instruction or advice if you cannot see the person climbing. It is also much more comforting for a nervous novice to be able to see and talk to the instructor.

Aim to have two good belays and do not hesitate to use peg belays if the natural ones are inadequate.

The amount of tension in the live rope when a student is climbing is quite important, slack gives a feeling of insecurity, can make a fall difficult to hold and imparts no 'feel' of what the student is doing. On the other hand a tight rope is uncomfortable and gives the student no true feeling of his balance. The happy medium is a rope which is just sufficiently taut to enable the instructor to feel the student as he moves. On the rare occasions when the stance does not permit a view of the pitch it is essential to maintain this correct tension as it is the only indication of how the student is progressing, particularly if conditions are difficult for communication.

Take a rucksack with the usual items of spare clothing, etc., plus a good first aid kit. Carry this with you on long routes or leave it in a place known to all the party at the foot of the cliff if the routes are reasonably short.

Occasionally an emergency situation may arise which cannot be solved without the instructor disengaging himself from the rope system. Such occasions should be few and far between if the instructor really knows his job, as one of the attributes of a good instructor should be the ability to recognize and avoid potentially awkward or dangerous situations. Many difficult situations in which inexperienced instructors find themselves are entirely of their own making and could have been avoided with a little foresight. An example which springs readily to mind is that of not telling the student to remove kinks from the rope when it is being taken in. The kinks, if bad, eventually jam in a runner and the leader can no longer keep the rope taut to the second. Things can go wrong, however, in the best-led parties and the instructor should possess the necessary technical skills and expertise to deal with any emergency which may arise. It is not within the scope of this book to describe the techniques necessary to cope with a complex emergency situation. These have been covered very adequately in *Improvised Techniques in Mountain Rescue* by Bill March. Those who are not confident of their abilities in this direction should practise the skills relating to freeing oneself from the rope system, rigging pulleys and friction brakes and the way to pass knots through the latter until they become second nature. Even then it is well to be aware that textbook situations seldom occur and that one should have the flexibility and ability to adapt the techniques to suit a particular situation.

Chapter Three

Mountain Rescue

Information on the theory and practice of mountain rescue is not readily available to the amateur mountaineer or to those who work in areas where accidents necessitating the use of sophisticated rescue equipment are rare. It has been found that many candidates for the Mountaineering Instructor's Certificate tend to be rather weak on the rescue section of the syllabus and for these reasons the syllabus requirements of the M.I.C. have been used as a basis for this chapter. These requirements are a knowledge of the following.

i The main causes of accidents.

ii Distress signals.

iii Action of party members, e.g. application of simple first aid, the four essentials of information, routine in exceptional circumstances.

iv Mountain rescue posts, police assistance, R.A.F. mountain rescue, first aid organizations and their function in the rescue service.

v Ability to organize a search and evacuation.

vi Knowledge of visual communication.

vii Familiarity with various stretchers, e.g. Thomas, Duff, McInnes, Mariner and the use of Thomas splints.

viii Ability to help with the evacuation of an injured climber from a cliff using an acceptable method.

ix Knowledge of other equipment such as types of illumination for night work, radios, etc.

x Mouth-to-mouth (nose) resuscitation.

xi Improvisation of rescue equipment.

1. The Main Causes of Accidents

The majority of accidents can be placed in three broad categories: lack of knowledge; overestimation of ability; carelessness.

Lack of knowledge covers a multitude of sins from the very simplest things such as knowledge of what boots and clothing to wear on the hills, what weather to expect and what to take with one, to complex and technical matters such as rope handling, winter equipment and techniques and good map reading. By far the greatest number of accidents can be placed in this category and anyone with an all-the-year-round knowledge of the hills can quote examples *ad nauseam* of the type of thing one is continually meeting when inexperienced parties are encountered. One of our aims as instructors is to try and impart this knowledge so that the future generations of mountaineers will not have to learn the hard way.

Overestimation of ability is inevitable with young, inexperienced rock climbers. Not content with their known limits they will push on beyond, a somewhat necessary trait if climbing standards are to continue to improve. Alas, some will always come unstuck, but of these the majority will escape unharmed due to their ability to protect themselves. The few who do not, become statistics in our accident records. Walkers, too, may overestimate their ability in terms of stamina or in the difficulties with which they consider themselves capable of dealing in their chosen route, particularly in bad weather conditions.

Carelessness may affect anyone. Novice and expert alike may have a careless moment and in fact the expert, due to his very expertise, may tend to have an accident caused by relaxation on what he considers to be easy ground. The classic example is the rock climber in P.A.s (Pierre Allains: a specialist, smooth rubber-soled, rock climbing boot) who, having completed a hard climb in dry conditions, descends an easy gully without giving it a thought. In doing so he steps on to a greasy slab in the shaded gully bed, slips and falls. It is unfortunate that in so doing he stands a much greater chance of serious injury than if he had fallen while on the climb and well protected. When falling off a steep rock climb the leader usually hits nothing and consequently damages nothing but his pride but when falling down easy, broken ground he will hit things frequently and subsequently suffer more injury. The great danger for the walker and mountaineer is a lack of awareness of the potential danger in a situation such as an apparently innocuous, convex grass slope in the rain. When wearing a full suit of waterproof plastic clothing a slip may be found hard to check and, given an unlucky combination of circumstances, the unfortunate walker falls over a cliff or steep drop hidden by the convexity and sustains an injury. The only constructive comment which one can make on carelessness is that one should try to develop an awareness of potential hazard and aim always to be careful when on a steep slope or over a drop, no matter how easy the place may appear to be.

2. Distress Signals

These should be common knowledge but as they have been revised fairly recently the new version is given below.

	Flare	*Sound*
Help wanted	Red	Six long whistle blasts, shouts, etc., *in quick succession*, a one-minute pause then repeat until answered.
Message understood	White (from party on hill)	Three long whistle blasts, etc., in quick succession, a one-minute pause then repeat.
Position of base	White or yellow, or white or yellow car headlights pointed upwards if possible.	
Recall to base	Green (used only at base)	A succession of notes on horn, bell or whistle, a succession of white or yellow lights switched on and off or a succession of thunderflashes.

The sound signal may also be given visually by heliograph or, at night, by torch or other visible means. It should also be remembered that parties in distress not knowing the system may signal S O S (three short, three long, three short signals).

3. Action of Party Members

When an accident occurs to a member of a party there is a sequence of actions which the party should take. These are as follows.

i Do not move the injured man unless you are well enough qualified in first aid to correctly diagnose his injuries. There is one important exception to this rule: if the person is unconscious he must be treated as described later in Chapter 4 and turned into the three-quarter prone position so that there is no chance of blood and vomit blocking his airway. Ignorance of this has led to many avoidable deaths, particularly in road accidents, where accident victims with minor facial injuries have been left face upward to literally drown in their own blood.

ii Give such first aid as you are able. With a normal first aid kit it should be possible to dress major open wounds, arrange a sling for a broken wrist or arm, make the patient comfortable and cover him with spare protective clothing. Improvised splints can be made but are not necessary if it is known that a fully equipped rescue team will be dealing with the casualty as they will be carrying much more efficient forms of splinting.

iii Send a message to the nearest rescue post giving the following four essential pieces of information.

a Location of the accident: name of cliff and climb or map marked to show the location. It is always better to send the map in preference to a grid reference as the latter is often reversed or otherwise incorrectly given by people in stress situations. If the accident is to a rock climber it is most important to state clearly whether the injured person is at the foot of the cliff or part-way up a climb as this will make a considerable difference to the personnel and equipment required by the rescue party.

b The number of people injured.

c The nature of the injuries.

d The time at which the accident took place.

The message should be written (it is useful to carry a piece of paper and a small pencil in the first aid kit for emergencies) and, if possible, should be taken by two people. If there are people in the party capable of helping with the carry this is useful information and should also be included in the message.

iv Prepare the area for the rescue team, i.e. remove loose stones, level a place for the stretcher (preferably at the head or foot of the patient so that the stretcher can be slid underneath as he is lifted rather than trying to move him sideways on to it, always a more difficult procedure), arrange good belays for the lower if necessary. If the accident site is at all difficult to locate spread out coloured anoraks around the area if conditions permit and if misty trail a rope across the hillside either side of the patient as a guide-line.

Circumstances are sometimes such that the above actions cannot be carried out in whole or part. For example the case may easily arise of an accident to a member of a party of inexperienced schoolchildren led by one member of staff. The teacher does not wish to leave the party alone nor does he want to send down any of the children with a message. Consider what your own actions would be in a situation such as this.

Each accident in the mountains demands its own solution and no really hard-and-fast rules can be laid down. It is in situations such as these that the skill, knowledge and resourcefulness of the person in charge of the party is tested to the full.

4. Mountain Rescue Posts, etc.

Full details of the organization of the Mountain Rescue Committee, the way in which rescue is organized in the British Isles and the distribution of the rescue posts are to be found in the booklet, *Mountain Rescue,* issued by the British Mountaineering Council.

Police assistance is always available if requested but the ability of the police to help in anything other than organization varies considerably from area to area. Mountaineers should know what to expect in the way of assistance and organization from the police in their own area.

The R.A.F. mountain rescue organization is intended solely for the rescue of survivors of aircraft accidents in the mountains and has no obligation to help with civilian accidents. However, in the best traditions of mountain rescue, they are always willing to help when called upon and are further able to be of great assistance by making available helicopters for search and rescue and by operating mobile radio links during large-scale search operations. Likewise civilian rescue teams are always prepared to assist with aircraft rescues.

The first aid organizations provide a countrywide network of courses to train people to an advanced level of first aid for general purposes but at the time of writing only one course exists (in North Wales) which is specifically aimed at the mountaineer and the problems of mountain first aid which differ considerably from those in the urban situation. Some of the members of the first aid organizations in mountain areas are very willing to help and are actively associated with rescue teams.

5. Ability to Organize a Search and Evacuation

Candidates should be familiar with the following aspects of search procedure.

i Quick searching of likely areas.

ii Use of dogs.

iii Division of the area to be screened into suitable search areas making use of natural boundaries.

iv Organization and composition of search parties.
v Methods of control.
vi Sweep searching and party searching.
vii Influence of weather conditions.
viii Siting of radio links.
ix Use of helicopters in search and evacuation.
x Other methods of evacuation.

6. Knowledge of Visual Communication

Basic knowledge of visual communication is given in section 2 of this chapter. This includes the use of flares, torches, etc. More advanced knowledge including methods of ground-to-air signalling is to be found in the training handbook for the R.A.F. mountain rescue teams.

7. Familiarity With Various Stretchers

Candidates should preferably have handled the main types of stretcher in use in this country and should be able to discuss their relative merits and shortcomings. The most commonly available stretcher is the Thomas (Pl. 13), which may also be obtained in split form for ease of carrying. This is the standard stretcher supplied to the majority of rescue posts in Britain. The MacInnes stretcher (Pl. 14a and 14b) is somewhat smaller and lighter than the Thomas and folds for carrying but tends to be a little less rigid in use. With its built-in headguard, lightness and ease of handling when folded it is a good stretcher to use in the evacuation of an injured climber from a cliff situation.

The Mariner (Pl. 15) is a continental stretcher with several interesting features, again folding and designed to run on a single wheel rather than be carried. It incorporates a good leg splint and method of applying traction and has a rigid, fibreglass bed unlike most British stretchers which utilize canvas, nylon or steel mesh beds. The Mariner is not in common use in this country.

Candidates should familiarize themselves with the setting up and handling of the Thomas and MacInnes stretchers and have at least a theoretical knowledge of the Mariner and other less common types, i.e. Perche-Bernard, Duff, Robertson. They should also have examined and used a Tragsitz (Pl. 16a and 16b) the device used to evacuate a climber with minor injuries from a cliff. For those living in areas where rescues are uncommon and specialized equipment not readily available the only way to gain a sound working knowledge of equipment and rescue methods is to attend a search and rescue course at one of the national centres.

8. Ability to Help With the Evacuation of an Injured Climber from a Cliff Using an Acceptable Method

This is normally taken to mean a rescue situation involving a long lower of more than one rope length using ordinary climbing equipment as opposed to specialized cliff rescue gear. A thorough knowledge of the following points is expected.

i Composition of the team.

ii Methods of getting the team and equipment to the accident site.

iii Stretcher loading under difficult conditions, i.e. on a small ledge.

iv Methods of attaching ropes to the stretcher for vertical and horizontal lowers.

v Improvised friction brakes and their application.

vi Lowering by body belays and the times when this method of lowering is to be preferred to the use of friction brakes.

vii Barrow boy, selection and security.

viii Co-ordination of the lower.

ix Changeover procedure at relay points.

x Passing a knot through a friction brake.

The work in this section forms a major part of the M.I.C. assessment for mountain rescue and it is invariably found that candidates are weak on the following points.

Working in a big cliff situation: Due to a lack of familiarity many people tend to be overimpressed by the location in which they may be called upon to carry out a rescue. To be efficient it is necessary to be at home in the situation which demands an abseil to reach the patient and examination, treatment, stretcher loading and lowering from a relatively small ledge in an exposed position. Personal safety in this kind of rescue situation is entirely the responsibility of each individual member of the team. Provided that one is at home on rock (which one should be at M.I.C. level) and that normal safety precautions are observed there should be no reason to feel ill at ease when faced with a cliff rescue.

Those who lack confidence should endeavour to get more practice in moving *down* big cliffs and in ways of safeguarding oneself adequately when working on small, exposed ledges.

Belaying: If anchors are to be used for direct lowering from friction brakes they must be absolutely beyond suspicion. Many people seem to lack awareness of this and fail either to make satisfactory peg placings or to find suitable anchors or are so slow as to give the impression that they do not really know what they are doing. Selection and use of anchor points must be quick and the results sound.

Friction brakes: A candidate should be able to rig a friction brake quickly and easily. All too often the impression given is that the operation is an unfamiliar one which has only been done at the most a few times before. Fluency can only be gained by practice. In addition the aspirant rescuer should be conversant with the method of passing a knot through a friction brake and with the back-up systems which can be used to maintain security against the possibility of the Mariner knot slipping while the transfer is being effected.

Attaching ropes to stretchers: The strong points of the stretcher in use should be known along with the best way of attaching ropes to them so that the load is well distributed. Ways of securing the patient should also be known and the variations necessary to deal with injuries such as a fractured pelvis.

The answer to most of the above problems is practice and more practice once the techniques have been learned. Rescue, particularly on cliffs, is a weakness of many candidates purely because they have had so little opportunity to handle the equipment and practise the techniques. A rescue course is an introduction, the techniques learned must be practised regularly if the required degree of proficiency is to be gained.

9. Knowledge of Other Equipment such as Types of Illumination for Night Work, Radios, etc.

Illumination for night work can be divided into personal, which will take the form of headlamps, and communal which is provided by some form of large, portable lamp.

Headlamps are essential for night rescue work as rescuers need both hands free. Most teams prefer battery-operated headlamps to those with rechargeable accumulators because of their lighter weight. Battery lamps will not run for so long as the accumulator type on one set of batteries, therefore a spare set and a spare bulb should be carried for each lamp.

Large, portable lamps giving excellent illumination may be obtained for night work, which run off compact accumulators of the same type as those for the headlamps. Lamps which run off gas may also be obtained but tend to form a rather bulky unit.

Portable (walkie-talkie) radios are of untold value in rescue work, particularly in the co-ordination of search and in maintaining contact between barrow boy and lowerers during a cliff rescue. However these alone are insufficient due to their limited range and also to the fact that they are likely to be screened from each other by intervening ridges, etc. A base set is required to maintain contact with the portables and to control their movements during a search or rescue operation. During a large-scale search in difficult country it may be necessary to set up links between base and portables to ensure contact with all parties. These links will normally be mobile base sets fitted in Land-Rovers, etc. Fig.2 shows a typical search communication network.

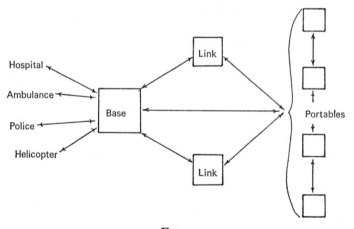

FIG. 2

All radio operators should have a knowledge of RT procedure otherwise chaos will ensue. Full details of this are given at the end of the chapter.

The type of portable radio most commonly used by British mountain rescue teams is the Pye Bantam which has a range of around 5 miles (8 km) and is battery operated. Spare batteries should always be carried when a set is in use. The base set is usually a Pye Cambridge which can be adapted to run from mains or car battery and can thus be used as mobile base or link when mounted in a suitable vehicle.

The radio frequency on which rescue sets operate is 86·325 MHz. Some cheap, Japanese sets are available but these operate on illegal frequencies. Usually they are of quite short range and may, in some circumstances, be used to control cliff lowers as a cheaper and lighter alternative to the Bantams.

Rescue equipment is constantly being developed and improved and it is obviously desirable that candidates should have up-to-date knowledge of equipment and methods. In particular, standard items of equipment for cliff lowers should be familiar. Prestretched terylene ropes, cables, friction brakes of various designs, winches, protection from falling stones and methods of evacuating cases of minor injury or exhaustion from cliffs need to be examined and evaluated.

10. Mouth-to-Mouth (Nose) Resuscitation
See *St John's Manual of First Aid*

11. Improvisation of Rescue Equipment

Full details of improvised rescue equipment and techniques are to be found in *Mountain Rescue Techniques* by Wastle Mariner and in *Improvised Techniques in Mountain Rescue* by Bill March. The relevant sections are clearly illustrated but require practice if they are to be utilized efficiently in an emergency. Particular attention should be given to the methods of setting up friction brakes, the addition of extra lengths of rope or cable while lowering and the construction of improvised stretchers and splints. Many people are conversant with the theory of rope stretchers, Dutch baskets, etc., but have obviously never carried anyone in them. When constructed they should be tested to see if they are efficient and if not why this is so. A common error is that of spacing the cross-lashings too far apart with the result that the patient is constantly slipping through the gaps.

Teaching Mountain Rescue

Mountain rescue teaching has something of value to offer both to the advanced student and to the teacher. The student gains not only experience in mountain rescue techniques but also increased confidence in moving about on cliffs and further much-needed practice in handling ropes, karabiners and other items of climbing equipment. The value to the instructor, particularly in areas where accidents are infrequent, is that he maintains a high level of competence in rescue organization and is able to deal efficiently with an emergency should it arise.

A certain amount of the work may be done equally well indoors or out and when the weather is fine the more done outside the better. The minimum theory which needs to be covered is the procedure in the event of an accident, dealt with elsewhere in this chapter, and the international code of distress signals. For the student who is an aspirant mountaineer this information will form an important part of the session. Those who are actively engaged in rescue work will know how infrequently one receives a model report of an accident and how much more difficult the task can become without the correct information. If all young mountaineers on completion of a course knew these basic essentials we would be a long way towards efficient rescue. If children are being introduced to rescue work the aim is usually to provide an imaginative, adventurous experience rather than to instil the basis of sound rescue, in which case the above theory and much of the detail of the practice can be omitted, but we are here considering those being taught rescue as part of a specialist rock climbing or mountaineering course.

Many of the following practical details can be taught indoors should the weather be really bad.

i Stretcher loading with particular emphasis on the handling of back injuries.

ii Attachment of ropes to the stretcher, knots, utilization of strong points and methods of spreading the load.

iii Friction devices and their limitations.

iv Ways of tying a harness for the barrow boy; triple bowline and bowline on a bight with a prusik loop for upper body support.

v The basic essentials of first aid may also be taught but this is better done as a separate, evening session.

Practical Work

Terrain: The ideal terrain for a first session involving stretcher lowering would be a small cliff, not more than 30 ft (9 m) in height, of easy angle and having a large, flat top with good belays. The latter point is essential so that the whole group may be assembled on the top of the cliff in safety and the stretcher loading and setting up of the lower can be carried out in ease with room to demonstrate and move about freely. Small ledges and exposed situations are advanced problems which should only be posed to groups who have a basic knowledge and competence.

Instruction: One instructor can safely handle a group of ten students given a good situation but only five students will be actively involved with any one lower, the others observing, helping to ease the stretcher over the edge of the cliff and acting as liaison between the lowerers and the barrow boy. If two instructors are available more activity can take place with a second group using a Tragsitz or trying a method of self-help such as a split-rope carry.

The first practical essential of a session is the examination of the available anchors, their suitability and a demonstration of how they should be linked together to give greater security. It is important that the students should realize the necessity for absolutely sound anchors when lowering from a friction device.

Lowering should at first be done using waist belays. This is the basic method of lowering a stretcher for short distances and has to be relied upon if the anchor points are not sufficiently sound for the use of friction brakes. Without experience of this type of lowering the student will be unable to appreciate the increased benefit to be obtained by the use of friction brakes. Gloves and protective clothing need to be worn when lowering from the waist and it is advisable that the stretcher first be lowered empty to give the students the feel of the situation without the full weight.

A difficulty with any type of lower is the co-ordination of the lowering party. Should one member of the team lower faster or slower than the rest the stretcher will tilt or the barrow boy will not move at the same speed as the stretcher which makes his task much more difficult. To achieve good co-ordination requires a considerable amount of practice but the situation is eased if the two outer lowerers face inward and try to lower at the same speed as the one in the centre. A further aid is to set up a system of signals by which the barrow boy can indicate when a particular rope is running faster or slower than the others. It may be necessary to have a man stationed on the edge of the ledge to relay the instructions from the barrow boy to the lowering group.

Friction brakes make the job of lowering physically much less demanding but have the limitation of being entirely dependent on the soundness of the anchorage. For this reason they must only be used when there is no question as to the strength of the anchors. The karabiner brake is the normal friction device used as it utilizes a common piece of equipment normally readily available in a rescue situation. During practice and wherever possible on rescues screwgate karabiners should be used throughout and the teacher should check every brake, every lower to ensure that it has been set up correctly. Peg/karabiner brakes should also be demonstrated using an angle peg as the bar. These are easier to set up than straight karabiner brakes and slightly more foolproof. A further alternative is to use a figure eight descendeur of the type now available in alloy. This is again a little easier to set up and gives slightly more braking effect than a single karabiner brake, in addition it can be very quickly locked off if the lower needs to be halted for any reason.

Lowers on a first session should be made with the stretcher in the vertical position. With more proficient groups the horizontal lower can be introduced. The bias in most rescue sessions appears to be towards stretcher lowering but some instruction needs to be given in the simple skills of stretcher carrying. The points which should be covered are.

i Choice of end men, tallest at the downhill end to attempt to level up the stretcher.

ii The method of holding the carrying straps and the correct adjustment of the end straps.

iii The ten man carry for transporting a heavy patient or when the carriers are children. (One extra man either side of the end man holding the stretcher handles.)

iv Route finding for the stretcher party.

v Methods of dealing with small drops and scree.

vi Descents of steep grassy slopes and snow.

vii Occasions where smoothness of carry is more important than speed and vice versa.

Advanced Rescue Techniques

Most courses are not of sufficient duration to go into rescue techniques in detail and many centres do not include rescue in the programme at all. The above outline of practical work would require a day for full coverage. Normally advanced work is covered by mountain rescue and search courses run at the national centres covering all aspects of the work but if more time could be devoted to rescue on a normal course it could be used to deal with search techniques, the use of radios, full-scale mock rescues on easy, one-pitch cliffs and instruction in big cliff rescues involving lowers of more than a rope length.

Organization

The organization of a rescue session is in many respects similar to that of a real rescue and again is good practice for the teacher in assembling the correct equipment. If friction brakes are to be used each one will require three screwgate karabiners or two plus an angle peg. There should be ample slings for belaying and a length of spare rope will be found useful for linking belays if they are widely separated. The lowering ropes get a lot of rough treatment in passing over edges of rock etc. under load and so ropes used for rescue practice should be old and kept solely for this purpose. They should be inspected regularly for damage.

If possible, a practice stretcher should be used for lowering as this saves a great deal of wear and tear on the rescue stretcher. The framework of any practice stretcher should be at least as strong as that of a normal stretcher so that ropes may be safely attached for lowering.

At all times during a practice lower the teacher in charge should be in a position to help the lowerers should any one of them start to lose control of his rope. He should also ascertain that everything is set up correctly and check all belays and knots before a lower commences.

Radio Telephony Procedure

Radio telephony (RT) communication makes co-ordination of a search or communication between barrow boy and lowering team on a big cliff very much easier. However, unless correct operating procedure is followed a great deal of confusion can arise.

Transmission requires a great deal more power than reception and therefore the operators should aim to keep transmissions as short as possible and speak clearly in order to avoid wastage of time and power by having to repeat messages.

When transmitting the following points will aid good communication.

i Speak across the microphone, not into it.

ii Remember RSVP:

Rhythm: Speak in short, complete phrases.

Speed: Do not speak too fast. Pause to allow important messages or numbers to be written down.

Volume: Speak louder than normal but do not shout. Try to avoid fading on the final word.

Pitch: Pitch your voice higher than usual as a higher pitch transmits better.

iii Good siting of sets will aid communication. 'Line of sight' positioning, where the view between sets is unobstructed, will give best results.

iv Intervening hills etc. will screen the sets causing loss of contact but VHF waves will 'bend' slightly and contact may often be regained by raising the set above the general surroundings. Often a small change in position will effect a great improvement.

Prowords Prowords are standard words which are used to abbreviate the routine statements which occur during a transmission. The use of prowords ensures that transmission time is kept to a minimum. A list of prowords and their meanings is given below.

OVER: My transmission is ended and I expect a reply from you. (**Never** use with OUT.)

OUT: End of transmission, no reply expected.

OUT TO YOU: End of my transmission to you. I am calling another station.

WAIT: Pause for a few seconds. Other stations do not transmit.

WAIT OUT: Pause of some duration. (Implication is that a later call will be made.)

RADIO CHECK or DO YOU READ: What is my signal strength and readability? (Answer: LOUD AND CLEAR, POOR or VERY WEAK.)

ROGER: Message received and understood.

WILCO: Message received and understood and I will comply with your instructions.

SAY AGAIN: Repeat your last transmission.

I SAY AGAIN: I am repeating my last transmission.

CORRECTION: Cancel last word and substitute . . .

NOTHING HEARD: Nothing heard.

FIGURES: Used before figures in content of message but not before call sign or grid reference.

GRID REFERENCE: Grid reference follows.

I SPELL: I shall spell the next word phonetically.

NEGATIVE: No.

AFFIRMATIVE: Yes.

MESSAGE FOR: Here is a message to be relayed to . . .

MESSAGE FROM: Here is a message from . . .

MESSAGE PASSED: The relay has been completed.

WORDS TWICE: Indicates that each word of the message will be repeated twice. Normally used when the signal strength is very weak.

Phonetic Spelling Occasionally a word has to be spelled out and to avoid ambiguity the phonetic alphabet is employed. This is given below together with the correct way to pronounce numbers.

A – Alpha	H – Hotel	O – Oscar	V – Victor
B – Bravo	I – India	P – Pappa	W – Whisky
C – Charlie	J – Juliet	Q – Quebec	X – X-ray
D – Delta	K – Kilo	R – Romeo	Y – Yankee
E – Echo	L – Lima	S – Sierra	Z – Zulu
F – Foxtrot	M – Mike	T – Tango	
G – Golf	N – November	U – Uniform	

Number Pronunciation

0 – Zero	3 – Thuh-Ree	6 – Six	9 – Nin-er
1 – Wun	4 – Fo-Wer	7 – Sev-en	10 – Wun Zero
2 – Too	5 – Fi-Yiv	8 – Ate	

Emphasis should be laid upon both syllables of those written as having two syllables. Two and three and five and nine are particularly prone to confusion on RT if this is not done.

RT Organization and Procedure Each post or team equipped with radio is given a call sign by the Mountain Rescue Committee, i.e. the Pen y Gwryd rescue post sign is PYG. The individual sets are further distinguished as follows: PYG CONTROL, PYG 1, PYG 2, PYG 3, etc. The control set is, as the name implies, usually a base set at the operation headquarters.

Control may arrange to send at set times and if so it is not necessary to switch on until about five minutes before call time, thus saving power. Otherwise sets should be kept on and each station should listen to all transmissions to avoid missing messages intended for them.

When calling, the name of the called station is given first in order to attract their attention, i.e. 'PYG I, this is PYG CONTROL.'

When communication is good Control may issue a collective call to all stations. Mobile stations reply in predetermined order giving their own call signs. Should one station fail to reply the next station in order should reply after a pause of thirty seconds.

Do not switch off unless told to do so by Control, he may wish to call you back.

The receiver may be faulty while the transmitter is still in working order and vice versa. Therefore one should continue to transmit if not receiving and keep listening if transmitter has failed.

The following example of RT procedure will illustrate the above. PYG Control is co-ordinating four mobile units in a search.

Establishment of communication. PYG Control this is PYG I. Over.

PYG I this is PYG Control. Over.

Name of called station omitted This is PYG I. Missing walker found at
when contact is firmly established. grid reference Six Wun Six Fi-Yiv Fi-Yiv Fo-Wer with broken ankle and slight exposure. Request stretcher and first aid kit. Over.

This is PYG Control. Wilco. Out.

Control now arranges for a standby party to take up the stretcher etc. then proceeds to call off the search.

Collective Call.

All stations this is PYG Control. Walker found, PYG 2, PYG 3, and PYG 4 return to base. Over.

PYG Control this is PYG I. Roger. Out.

PYG Control this is PYG 2. Roger. Out.

No reply from PYG 3, a pause of thirty seconds then:

PYG Control this is PYG 4. Say Again. Over.

This is PYG Control, I say again, walker found return to base. Over.

This is PYG 4. Roger. Out.

Control now tries again to contact PYG 3.

> PYG 3 this is PYG Control. Over.

Still no reply. Control thinks that 2 is in a better position to establish contact.

> PYG 2 this is PYG Control. Relay message to PYG 3. Over.
>
> This is PYG 2. Wilco. Out to you. PYG 3 this is PYG 2. Over.
>
> PYG 2 this is PYG 3. Over.
>
> This is PYG 2. Message from Control, walker found return to base. Over.
>
> This is PYG 3. Roger. Out.
>
> PYG Control this is PYG 2. Message passed. Over.
>
> This is PYG Control. Roger. Out.

Chapter Four

First Aid

Every person intending to take organized parties into the mountains should have a reasonable knowledge of first aid procedures to enable him to deal with minor emergencies and to aid him in taking the correct course of action if faced with a serious accident. Those intending to take the M.I.C. must hold an up-to-date adult first aid certificate of the St. John's Ambulance Brigade, Red Cross or St. Andrew's Ambulance Association as a minimum requirement.

Courses for the purpose of gaining this qualification are held every winter in most large towns and cities. Admirable as these courses are, they are not intended for the mountaineer but for the person who may be called upon to deal with an accident in everyday life where, normally, qualified medical help is close at hand. The situation with regard to mountain accidents presents a much more complicated problem. Accidents often take place in remote areas where the patient may have to be carried for several hours over difficult terrain before he can be brought within reach of expert medical aid. In such situations the first aid man carries more responsibility and, to give adequate help, needs to have more detailed knowledge of the diagnosis and treatment of injuries than that gained on the normal first aid course. He must also be able to correlate this knowledge with the mountaineering problems involved in order to arrive at the correct decisions regarding treatment and evacuation of the patient.

At the time of writing only one course is known to exist which caters specifically for mountain first aid. This is run under the auspices of the St John's Ambulance Brigade by Dr Ieuan Jones, Senior Accident Officer at the Caernarvonshire and Anglesey Hospital, Bangor, himself a keen mountaineer and medical adviser to all the local mountain rescue teams. Since the inception of this course the standard of first aid in the mountains of Snowdonia has improved considerably and, thanks to the untiring efforts of Dr Jones, there is a degree of co-ordination between rescue teams, ambulance men and the hospital accident unit which exists nowhere else in the country. Ideally every interested mountaineer in the country should have the opportunity of attending such a course but obviously this is not possible at present.

The purpose of this chapter is not to present a potted first aid course but to try and draw attention to some of the aspects of first aid which are pertinent to the mountaineer but which are not fully dealt with in the first aid manuals. I hope that those with a basic first aid knowledge will find the following notes useful in familiarizing them with the more specialized aspects and problems of first aid in mountaineering. The accompanying diagrams are meant to be schematic rather than anatomically correct.

Examination and Diagnosis

The inherent weakness in the person with some knowledge of first aid lies in the fact that he does not know how to examine a patient thoroughly and quickly. The tendency is to see and concentrate on the obvious injury while the less obvious (and perhaps more serious) injury goes undetected. Where mountain accidents are concerned the more detailed the diagnosis of the patient's injuries the better, as all decisions regarding mode of transport, speed of evacuation and on-the-spot treatment will be based on this information. Having arrived at the scene of the accident and, if necessary, secured himself and the patient, the first aid man should follow the sequence given below in order to make a thorough check of the condition of the patient.

Order of Examination
i Check first that the patient is breathing, has a clear airway and has no severe haemorrhage. Treat immediately if any of these are present. (Details of the treatment for this and the examination of the spine are given later in the chapter.)
ii Check for fractured spine and other major breaks before attempting to move to a more suitable location for further examination and treatment should the patient be in a very awkward place. If spinal or other major injuries are found it is advisable not to attempt to move the patient unless he is in immediate danger from stonefall, avalanche, etc. but to carry out the rest of the examination as best one can on the spot.
iii Detailed examination: always start at the head and work methodi-

cally down the body to the feet using both hands simultaneously on opposite sides of the body for comparison. In this way no injury reasonably obvious to the layman will be missed and the use of both hands will help to reveal discrepancies between injured and normal limbs, i.e. swelling or deformity. Talking to the patient will help considerably. It will, of course, immediately reveal the level of consciousness and if the patient is fully conscious he will be able to co-operate by indicating areas of pain during the examination. Step-by-step examination is better seen than described but the following notes should be found useful.

a Slip a hand under the lowest point of the head. If blood is found a further check for head wounds should be made. If no blood is found it is unlikely that there are scalp wounds of any significance.

b Run the fingers firmly over the scalp, feeling for depressions and on over the bony promontories of the cheeks, nose and line of the jaw.

c Try to feel the bony prominences of the neck from the base of the skull down to the shoulder line. Swelling and pain may indicate a broken neck.

d Look for blood or clear fluid emerging from the ears or nose. If found wipe clean and see if it re-appears to establish whether it has in fact come from the ear or nose or whether it has come from another wound. Bleeding from the ear is an indication of a fracture of the base of the skull and from the nose an indication of a fracture of the front of the skull.

e Look at the eyes and compare pupil sizes. Unequal pupils and no reaction to light are signs of compression of the brain due to a generalized injury to the skull. Formation of a black eye or bleeding into the white of the eye are further signs of a frontal fracture of the skull.

f Run your fingers along the collar bones, round the shoulders and down the arms checking the upper arm (humerus), bony points of the elbow (there should be three, forming a triangle when the elbow is bent) and forearms. Take the pulse at the wrist. A very slow pulse (below 60) is a further indication of cerebral compression. A fast and feeble pulse indicates shock. Clench the hands lightly in your own to check for broken fingers.

g Place your hands flat on the rib cage and try to feel and see the motion of the chest when breathing. Reciprocal breathing (one part of the chest going in when the rest is coming out) is an indication of a flail segment, a serious chest injury in which several ribs are broken in more than one place (Fig. 3). Frontal pressure on the rib cage will indicate, in a conscious patient, any areas of pain which may be bruises or fractures. If fairly firm pressure inwards from the sides gives rise to pain in the same spot a fracture may be assumed.

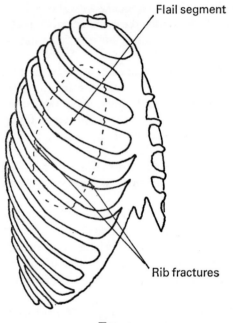

Flail segment

Rib fractures

FIG. 3

h The abdomen may be divided into four quadrants by imagining lines drawn horizontally and vertically through the navel. Place a hand flat in each quadrant in turn, fingers pointing towards the navel and, using all the fingers, depress the abdomen gently. Normally it is flaccid but in the event of an internal abdominal injury the abdominal muscles contract and the abdomen will feel rigid and possibly tender.

Internal abdominal injuries are not easy to detect as there is no obvious external injury and the patient may be aware of little or no pain and this, if present, may be masked by other more painful injuries. If one suspects an injury of this nature check also for clothing or rope marks on the abdomen indicating a forceful blow. There is a great deal of haemorrhage from an internal abdominal injury and the patient will be deeply shocked. Signs of shock with no other serious wounds to account for it should lead one to suspect this type of injury.

i Press gently on the pubis. If there is any pain or tenderness assume a fractured pelvis and do not proceed any further with the pelvic examination. If this action causes no pain at this stage press inwards on the sides of the pelvis. Again pain is an indication of a fracture. It is extremely important that this part of the examination is carried out in correct sequence for a fractured pelvis, if pressed from the side first, can in some circumstances trap and perforate the bladder. If there is a possibility that the bladder has been injured (or pelvis crushed) it is advisable that the patient should not pass water, as the attempt may cause urine to leak into the abdomen and cause infection.

j Run the hands down the thighs (femurs), feel above the knee-caps, the knees themselves and just below for swelling. Swelling at these points would be an indication, in turn, of a fracture of the lower end of the femur, damage to the knee-joint or knee-cap and a fracture of the upper end of the shin bone (tibia). Continue on down the shin to the ankle feeling the bony prominences at either side.

k Tap the bottom of each heel. Pain here is an indication not only of possible fractured bone of the heel but also of a possible compression fracture of the spine, particularly if the patient is known to have landed on his feet on level ground.

l To examine the spine turn the patient away from yourself taking great care not to twist him in the process or to bend the spine. Unless the technique of doing this is known it is advisable to get help when turning the patient. Lift the patient's clothing sufficiently to be able to feel the bony prominences from the neck down to the pelvis. Areas of swelling or displacement may be felt coupled with pain or tenderness if a fracture is present. While the patient is in this position check for broken shoulder blades and any tenderness around the loins indicating possible kidney damage. There may also be rib fractures at the back.

If the above method of examination is practised and closely adhered to very little will go unnoticed. However a knowledge of the commoner types of injury which tend to occur in mountain accidents will help to ensure an accurate diagnosis. This is essential if the correct treatment is to be given and the best method of transport employed. Detailed information regarding this is beyond the scope of this chapter but the main points will now be considered.

Head Injuries

These can be divided into two catagories: *local* in which the damage is confined to a small area, due perhaps to a blow on a sharp rock, and *generalized* in which the impact has been spread over a large area of the skull causing the brain to hit the inside of the skull. If severe, this jarring leads to bruising and consequent swelling of the brain which becomes compressed as it has very little room in which to expand. A slight injury of this type leads to *concussion* with which there may be an initial loss of consciousness followed by recovery, probably accompanied by headache. Severe injury resulting in *compression* is indicated by the patient becoming more deeply unconscious, a slowing pulse rate and inequality of the pupils of the eyes with diminished reaction to light. Breathing may become slow and noisy due to the respiratory centre in the brain being affected by the compression.

Treatment If the patient is unconscious the airway must be checked immediately and, if necessary, cleared. He should never be left face upwards as this allows blood and vomit to block the airway but should be turned into the three-quarter prone position (Pl. 17). This position should be maintained by a firm pad under the chest and allows all secretions to drain from the mouth and nose. A careful watch should be kept on the breathing, and every half-hour a check should be made on the level of consciousness, pulse rate and pupil size. The following terms are useful in describing level of consciousness; talkative, quiet, drowsy, rousable, responds to simple commands, reacts to painful stimulus, does not respond to any stimuli. This half-hourly check may help to confirm the initial diagnosis and the information gained on the change in the condition of the patient may be of value when he reaches hospital, i.e. if a patient with a head injury is talkative when reached, is drowsy half an hour later and a further half-hour later reacts only to a painful stimulus his level of consciousness is deepening indicating compression, but the reverse would indicate concussion. Rapid onset of compression symptoms is serious and calls for urgency in transport to hospital.

Scalp wounds should be covered with a sterile, absorbent pad and bandaged firmly as they tend to bleed freely. No morphia should be given if the patient is unconscious *or has been unconscious.*

Stretcher carrying and lowering is carried out in the normal way with conscious patients but in the case of the unconscious patient, the stretcher should be lowered in a horizontal position and, when being carried, horizontal or even slightly head-down position should be maintained.

Spinal Injuries

Any pain or swelling in the mid-line of the back should be taken as indication of spinal injury and treated as such. All spinal injuries, including neck, should be treated as extremely serious. There should be no hurry during the rescue operation and all handling should be very gentle. It is of vital importance that the patient is not bent forward or twisted when being put on to the stretcher. He should be lifted by as many people as possible acting in unison. The hands are passed underneath his body and all lift slowly at a word of command, aiming to avoid flexion or rotation of the spine. The stretcher is passed underneath from the head or the foot and the patient is placed on it face-down to maintain the correct spinal curve. Any stretcher lowering should be horizontal and carrying should be smooth and unhurried.

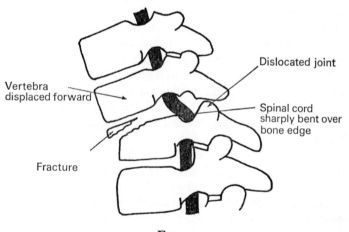

Vertebra displaced forward

Dislocated joint

Spinal cord sharply bent over bone edge

Fracture

FIG. 4

Although it is fairly common knowledge that back injuries require careful handling very few people really know why. Fig. 4 shows a section of the spinal column at the site of a fracture/dislocation, the most serious spinal injury. It will be noticed that a sharp edge of bone is pressed against the spinal cord and that any forward flexion or rotation of the spine could cause the bone edge to sever the cord.

Morphia may be given for spinal injuries except those of the neck as one of the side-effects of morphia is to induce vomiting in many cases. This could be fatal in the case of a neck injury and patients with back injuries should also be warned not to make any sudden movements should they wish to vomit.

Chest Injuries

The most common chest injuries are bruising and fractures of the ribs but these can be complicated by lung damage from a broken rib, indicated by frothy blood at the mouth, or by penetration of the chest from without causing a sucking wound. If present this should be sealed by a large, sterile dressing otherwise breathing will be seriously impaired. If lung damage is diagnosed the patient should be tilted slightly towards the injured side to keep the blood away from the undamaged lung, the action of which could be impaired by the build-up of blood in the chest cavity.

The most serious chest injury is known as a flail segment. This is caused by several ribs being broken in two or more places so that a section of the chest wall does not move with the rest when breathing but in fact moves in the opposite direction, i.e. when the patient breathes in the flail section is sucked inward as the chest wall expands. The best emergency treatment of this is immobilization by fixing a large pad firmly over the flail segment with long strips of adhesive strapping passed well round the chest but not completely encircling it. The aim should be to fix the segment in the 'in' position, i.e. when the patient has inhaled.

Morphia should not be given for chest injuries as one of the side-effects is to depress the breathing. In serious injuries to the chest breathing may already be impaired and a careful watch on respiration should be maintained. If other injuries permit, the patient may feel better if transported in a sitting position. This poses carrying problems. Some support may be arranged by using a frame rucksack but even better is the big basket headguard designed for the Thomas stretcher. If one of these is available it makes a very good support for a sitting patient if reversed. A sitting patient will be very unstable to carry and extra supporters may be necessary on either side of him in addition to the normal carriers.

Abdominal Injuries

Open wounds of the abdomen should be covered with a sterile dressing and if any foreign body is present this should be removed. Closed injuries of the abdomen are hard to detect and may be very serious. Severe shock without any obvious injuries elsewhere should lead one to suspect abdominal injury. The muscles of the abdomen will be rigid and there will probably be slight pain which may be masked by other more painful, but less serious, injuries. No treatment can be given on the hill and the patient should be transported to hospital as quickly as possible.

Morphia should not be given for abdominal injuries as this will mask the symptoms on which the decision to operate will have to be made.

Fractures of the Upper Limbs

Most upper limb fractures are not too serious with the exception of those in the area of the elbow joint. Fig. 5 shows the joint area normal and when damaged by a fracture of the lower end of the humerus. It can immediately be seen that mishandling could result in damage to the brachial artery.

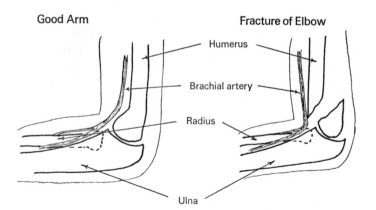

FIG. 5

When this type of injury is present the arm should be kept in the position in which it is found. Plastic inflatable splints are unsuitable for this injury which should be immobilized with a Kramer wire splint well padded and bent to the shape of the arm. The arm should be firmly bandaged to the splint and then secured to the side of the chest with broad bandages above and below the break. Before bandaging is completed the radial pulse should be checked at the wrist to ensure that the artery has not been trapped while splinting.

Fractures of the Lower Limbs

Most lower limb fractures, with the exception of the femur, are best splinted with a full-leg plastic inflatable splint if there is little deformity. The femur should be immobilized with a Thomas leg iron which can be used to apply traction if necessary. A considerable amount of blood will be lost into the body tissues from a broken femur, resulting in a high degree of shock. Morphia should be given unless other injuries, e.g. head, prevent this. It can also be given for major breaks of the lower leg if severe pain and shock are present.

Bleeding

Serious arterial bleeding is seldom encountered in mountain accidents and will only be of concern to those immediately in the vicinity at the time of the accident. Direct pressure on the wound and elevation will control arterial bleeding. On no account should a tourniquet be used.

All other open wounds should be covered with a large, sterile, absorbent pad bandaged firmly in place but not so tightly as to impair circulation. As a general rule foreign bodies should be left in all wounds except those of the abdomen.

Shock

The term shock is commonly used to imply a mental or nervous condition. Although this may be present in a patient, due to worry about his injuries, etc., the type of shock with which we are mainly concerned in mountain accidents is physical in origin, largely due to loss of blood, and can lead to death if not treated. It can be caused by haemorrhage from wounds, fractures of major bones and internal injuries. The loss of blood may be entirely internal – into the tissues, without a drop of blood appearing on the surface. Shock can also result from natural causes such as heart attack. It is nearly always present to some degree in accident cases and is indicated by the 'Three Ps': pulse – fast and weak; perspiration – cold; and pallor – yellowish white.

Treatment of shock is a task for the hospital, requiring blood trans-fusion, and the rescuer's job is to try to delay its development. This may be achieved by controlling heavy bleeding, the administration of morphia if no contra-indications are present (preferably within twenty minutes of the accident taking place if it is to be really effective) and by keeping the patient cool but above the temperature at which he com-mences to shiver.

Exposure

Rescue teams are often called out to deal with cases of exposure and all mountaineers should familiarize themselves with the causes, prevention and treatment of this condition. This is fully dealt with in the B.M.C. pamphlet No. 380 but the main causes and basic treatment are set out below.

The term exposure implies, in this context, exposure to inclement weather conditions, particularly wet cold. If the mountaineer is not suitably clad and nourished or in such a situation fails to seek shelter, a progressive drop in body temperature will occur. The body defence mechanism will attempt to maintain the temperature of the brain and vital organs (known collectively as 'the core') at $98.4°$ F ($37°$ C), but if it drops much below this there is a rapid physical and mental deterioration followed by collapse, coma and, unless the correct emergency treatment is quickly given, death.

It is most important that the core temperature should not drop any lower and to prevent further heat loss the patient should be sheltered from the cause of the exposure by whatever means are available on the spot. Ideally a tent should be erected and the patient placed within this in a sleeping bag while a rescue party is summoned. No external rubbing, application of hot water-bottles or alcohol should be given as these tend to increase the circulation in the cold outer shell of skin and muscle. Such action cools the blood still further which in turn reduces the core temperature, often with fatal results. If the clothing of the patient is sodden, rather than stripping and replacing with dry clothing it is better to place him in a polythene bag and then the sleeping bag so that the insulation of the latter is not affected. If a tent is not available the sleeping bag should then be protected by a further polythene bag and the patient placed in a sheltered, slightly head-down position.

If he is conscious the patient may be given hot liquids and quick energy foods such as glucose, Kendal mint cake, etc. The rescue party should carry the patient (even if apparently recovered) quickly to base, endeavouring to maintain insulation from the elements at all costs. The carry is best done with the patient in a slightly head-down position. An unconscious patient is in a critical condition and preferably should not be transported but should be sheltered as indicated above until there is some improvement in his condition or until a doctor arrives.

When at base a hot bath, between 108° and 112° F (42° and 44° C), should be prepared and the patient placed in this. Indication of recovery should be evident in about 10–20 minutes and when the patient begins to sweat it can be considered safe to transfer him to a warm room at a temperature of about 70° F (20° C). If at all possible a doctor should be present during the rewarming as patients in an advanced state of hypothermia pass through a critical stage in the process where it is possible for heart failure to occur, but speed is essential and if a doctor is not standing by when the patient arrives it is best to commence the treatment.

Frostbite

Frostbite is caused by actual freezing of the tissues and does not occur above temperatures of around 30° F (−1° C). As the blood supply to the extremities is reduced in cold conditions, in order to maintain the core at its correct temperature, fingers and toes are particularly susceptible to frostbite unless adequately insulated. Due to the difficulty of protecting them, cheeks, nose and to a certain extent ears, are also areas commonly affected. For the purpose of treatment frostbite may be divided into two categories: *superficial* frostbite in which the affected tissue is white but still soft when pressed and *deep* frostbite where the exposure to severe cold has been prolonged and the tissues feel solid and cannot be depressed.

Superficial frostbite is the most common and the best treatment is rewarming in the field by placing the affected part against a warmer part of the body, i.e. frostbitten fingers may be placed in the armpit or in the mouth. Rubbing the affected part should never be resorted to as this is harmful. Ideally it is better to rewarm hands and feet before they become frostbitten, the danger signs being the pain of intense cold followed by loss of sensation. In very low temperatures, not often encountered in Britain, it is easy to develop patches of superficial frostbite on cheeks or nose without them being noticed. Members of parties in such conditions should keep a check on each other to prevent this happening. Once rewarmed every effort should be made to keep the affected part warm as it is most harmful to allow the same area to become frostbitten again.

Deep frostbite should always be left until it is possible to treat in hospital or at a base where there are adequate facilities and no chance of subsequent refreezing. Delay in rewarming is far less harmful than rewarming followed by refreezing and it is important to bear in mind in mountaineering and winter travelling situations that whereas it is possible to walk on frozen feet it is not possible to walk on feet which have been thawed. Treatment of deep frostbite is by rapid rewarming of the affected part by immersion in water kept accurately at $108°$ to $112°$ F ($42°$ to $44°$ C) until it is thawed which will normally take at least twenty minutes. When rewarmed the injured part should be kept warm, left uncovered and exposed to the air.

Burns

Burns and scalds are a potential hazard when camping. Mostly these are of a minor nature but they could, in the case of a tent fire or a gas stove explosion, be quite serious.

Burns may be classified as superficial or deep and large or small. Superficial burns may exhibit red or blistered skin and are extremely painful. All scalds and blistered burns may be regarded as superficial. In deep burns the skin may be charred and the tissue beneath also destroyed. Deep burns may be less painful than superficial if the nerve endings have been destroyed.

If expert medical treatment is not obtainable reasonably quickly the size of the burn becomes an important factor due to the development of burn shock caused by loss of body fluids from the surface of the wound. Any burn which covers 18 per cent or more of the body surface area is considered to be a large burn and presents a risk to life. An idea of the area of the burn can be gained from what is known as the rule of nines which is determined by considering the major areas of the body in multiples of 9 per cent as follows; head and neck 9 per cent each, arm 9 per cent, front torso 18 per cent, back torso 18 per cent, each leg 18 per cent. If conscious any victim with large burns should be given plenty to drink in small, frequent quantities. Aim to give 2 fluid ounces (57 cc) per 9 per cent of burnt area every twenty minutes for the first eight hours to offset the fluid loss from the burned area.

Burns should be left exposed to the air or covered with a sterile, absorbent gauze dressing. Burn creams etc. should not be applied and as the burned surface is sterile it is best left untouched other than to remove loose, burned clothing. The aim should be to keep the surface free from any further contamination until medical help is available. In the case of rope burns resulting from a rock climbing accident or other small burns these can be covered with a tulle dressing if available but otherwise treat as above.

Lightning

Lightning injuries are not common, even on mountains, but are frequent enough to warrant attention. In Britain around eight people die each year as a result of being struck by lightning. When struck a person receives a severe electric shock and treatment is thus the same as that given for the more conventional severe electrical injuries. A person struck by lightning usually exhibits characteristic fern-like burns. A direct strike on the head, earthing at the feet via the brain and heart, stops both heart and breathing and is usually fatal. A strike earthing from hand to foot via the heart causes the heart to fibrillate and no heartbeat will be detectable. Breathing ceases with the initial shock but should recommence spontaneously within 2 to 3 minutes and the treatment should be directed towards making the heart function normally. An initial hard blow on the sternum may induce a normal heartbeat but, if not, it should be followed by external cardiac massage. If breathing does not recommence within 2 to 3 minutes mouth-to-mouth artificial respiration should also be given. Once started these measures should be continued until recovery or until the victim is declared dead.

Illnesses

Any person taking parties on to the hills may have to deal with an emergency situation brought about by the illness of a member of the group. A basic knowledge of the signs and symptoms and treatment of the ones most commonly encountered is invaluable.

Epilepsy An epileptic fit is a frightening experience for all concerned and the main aim of the other members of the party should be to prevent the patient injuring himself by the violence of his movements, particularly in a situation where a fall could result from his actions. In this situation helpers should also pay attention to their own safety while dealing with the patient. After the attack the patient should be allowed to recover and then encouraged to make his way down slowly with assistance. He should be watched carefully after apparent recovery as he may be in a state of automatism, i.e. not fully aware of his actions, but it is not normally necessary or desirable to evacuate him by stretcher.

Diabetes Diabetics may go into an insulin coma during a day on the hills if they are inexperienced and fail to make allowances in their diet for the extra energy expenditure, thus using up their bodily reserves of sugar. This may also occur if the day is prolonged by unforeseen circumstances. When this happens they become excitable, hot, sweaty and drowsy suddenly and should be given sugar in quantity before they become unconscious. Often a diabetic will carry a reserve of lump sugar with him and should also be given hot sweet drinks. A feature of the onset of insulin coma is that often the sufferer becomes confused and aggressive. He may refuse the sugar, etc. and has to be forced to take it.

Asthma Experienced mountaineers who are asthmatic very seldom suffer attacks on the mountains, but novices who find themselves in a stress situation are more susceptible as the condition is provoked by stress. Breathing becomes difficult and wheezy and the sufferer becomes frightened. This in turn can lead to a further deterioration in the breathing. Usually it is sufficient to reassure the patient, relieve the stress situation by removing him from the danger, real or imagined, and allow him to recover. If he has tablets or other treatment with him this should be used. When sufficiently recovered he should be able to make his way down without the necessity of being carried.

Appendicitis This is indicated by tenderness at McBurney's point which lies approximately one-third of the distance between the bony prominence at the front of the right hip and the navel. The abdomen may be locally rigid but if the whole of the abdomen is rigid the more serious condition of peritonitis may be present. The patient will have a high pulse rate, in the region of 100–110, a dry mouth and coated tongue.

Perforated Ulcer This will also result in symptoms similar to appendicitis. The patient will be very shocked and lying very still with the abdomen rigid. Both appendicitis and perforated ulcer are serious and require immediate, speedy evacuation.

Coronary Thrombosis In the mountaineering context this is likely to be encountered in the 40 to 50 age group. Following exertion the person complains of pain in the chest or indigestion, stops for a rest and collapses. If he survives the attack he will be very pale with a bluish tinge to the lips and ears, in a cold sweat and may have difficulty in breathing. There will be severe pain under the lower sternum and possibly up to the left shoulder and left arm.

It is most important that the patient does not exert himself in any way. He should be reassured, made comfortable, tight clothing loosened and told to relax completely to avoid any more strain on the heart. Morphia should be given if the diagnosis is certain. Transport should be slow and gentle with particular care taken when lifting on to the stretcher.

With an unconscious patient cardiac massage should be given immediately a stoppage of the heart is noticed and continued until recovery or until the patient is pronounced dead. It may also be necessary to give artificial respiration should the breathing also cease.

Death

Only a doctor can officially certify death but it can be of value to rescuers to know how to diagnose whether a victim is dead. If, for example, a casualty is found after a search, late at night and in difficult terrain, it will usually be decided to bring him down in daylight if he is dead to avoid subjecting rescuers to unnecessary risks but, if he is alive and injured, rescuers will make every effort to get him down quickly despite the hazardous conditions.

The following signs will always be present if a person is dead: no detectable pulse or heartbeat; no breathing; pupils of the eyes will not react to light and will be dilated. When the patient has been dead for some time the following signs may be found: the blood will have drained to the lower part of the body in relation to the position in which he is lying, causing a bluish discoloration of the skin called *lividity*. Rigor mortis may have set in.

It is also quite possible that, in the case of mountain accidents, in addition to the above symptoms, the victim may have injuries which obviously preclude any chance of his being alive.

Analgesics

The analgesic most commonly available to mountain rescue teams is morphia which is packed in tubonic ampoules. These consist of a dose of morphia in a tube rather like a miniature toothpaste tube to which is attached a short hypodermic needle. To make it ready for use the person administering the injection merely has to remove the ampoule from its sterile container and break the seal in the needle with the stilette provided. The dosage contained in the ampoule is morphia $\frac{1}{4}$ grain or Omnopon $\frac{1}{3}$ grain which contains morphia $\frac{1}{6}$ grain.

Other analgesics, the most promising of which appears to be Fortral, are now considered by many people to be superior to morphia as the side-effects are not so severe while the benefits are about the same. In addition Fortral is non-habit forming. Because of the lesser side-effects, analgesics such as Fortral can be used for a larger variety of injuries than morphia. Unfortunately these analgesics are not obtainable in ampoule form and therefore of necessity they have to be administered by those trained in the use of a hypodermic syringe, and it is unlikely that they will be freely available for use in mountain accidents in the near future. For this reason the only analgesic which has been considered in the text is morphia. A summary of its actions and occasions on which it should or should not be used is given below.

Actions of Morphia
i It slows the development of shock.
ii It relieves pain.
iii It induces sleep.
iv It is likely to cause vomiting in about one-third of those to whom it is given.

v It causes the pupils of the eyes to constrict.
vi It lowers the blood pressure.
vii It depresses respiration.

Morphia Should Be Given For:
i Major fractures, i.e. spine, femur, tibia, pelvis.
ii Dislocation of the shoulder or hip-joints.
iii Multiple injuries (but excluding head and neck fractures, and abdominal injuries).
iv Coronary thrombosis.

Morphia Should Not Be Given:
i For serious head injuries, i.e. fractured skull, or to a person who has been unconscious for more than a few seconds or to a person who is unconscious.
ii Where there is any condition causing difficulty of breathing or shortness of breath.
iii Fractures of the neck. The dangerous consequences of vomiting outweigh the beneficial effects of the morphia.
iv In cases of exposure and exhaustion.
v If the patient is known to be taking tranquillizers.
vi Abdominal injuries.

Administration *Whatever the nature of the injuries morphia should not be given if any of the above contra-indications are present.* To be most effective it is best administered within twenty minutes of the accident taking place. If necessary the dosage may be repeated every four hours. The normal dose is one tubonic ampoule for adults and half for those under fourteen years of age or over seventy. None should be given to children under the age of seven. Instructions for administration, which is subcutaneous, are supplied with each pack and are easy to understand but the following points should be noted.
i Make sure that the seal has been broken before throwing away the stilette.
ii Usually the most accessible sites for the injection are the forearm and the stomach, of these the former is to be preferred.
iii The needle should be introduced quickly and forcibly if the patient is to suffer minimum discomfort.
iv Make sure that all the contents are expelled from the tube before withdrawing the needle.

v Keep the empty tube, some teams like to have them back in order to verify use and obtain fresh supplies.

vi When the dose has been given pin a note on to the garments of the patient in a conspicuous position stating what dose has been given and at what time. In addition make a point of passing this information on to the ambulance men.

Chapter Five

Hillcraft

Of all the aspects of mountaineering, hillcraft – general movement over mountains and the ability to do this with competence – is perhaps the most deceptive. Compared to the technicalities of rock climbing, snow- and icework or skiing a walk in the mountains appears to be a simple and straightforward matter. However, this is certainly not substantiated by accident reports. Accidents to walking parties have always been more frequent than those to rock climbers and recent accident figures show a trend towards a further increase in the former and decrease in the latter. To ascertain exactly why this should be so would require a very detailed study of the accident reports over a number of years but it can safely be said that a number of accidents are due to the fact that many people are misled by the apparent simplicity of mountain walking and lack an awareness of the dangers inherent in mountain country.

Good hillcraft is a basic requirement for anyone engaged in work in outdoor activities whether as a permanent instructor or in a part-time capacity within the school or youth service situation. Not only should he have wide experience of a number of mountain areas at all times of the year coupled with stamina, hillsense and a thorough understanding of navigation but the good teacher needs to have the ability to make a day in the mountains interesting and enjoyable whatever the conditions. A successful mountain day is not necessarily measured by the number of summits reached but by what the party gained from the day and how much enjoyment they had. This is by no means an easy task. Mountain walking can be, and often is, downright boring for a group of school-children if it is not presented in the right way. The group of brightly waterproof-clad figures plodding miserably up into the mist and rain behind an instructor is a common sight in our more popular mountain areas and it is very hard to provide any logical answer to the inevitable question, 'Why are we going up here in the rain and cold with nothing to see?' Walking lacks the built-in excitement of rock climbing and canoe-ing and it is up to the teacher to provide the stimulus which will turn a plod into an interesting day. How he achieves this will depend upon a number of factors: his personality, manner and contact with the group all have an important bearing. Knowledge of the area is essential if he is to be able to utilize the points of interest *en route* to their full advantage, and the more aware he is of the environment the more likely it is that he will be able to exploit to the full the teaching opportunities which a mountain day provides. The instructor with a fund of knowledge about birds, animals, plants, rocks and local legends and stories is usually the one who will bring back a happy group. Choice of terrain to suit the party is another factor which can contribute largely to the success of the day.

There is no set formula for making a mountain day a good one, but there is plenty of scope for each individual to develop the day in a way which will enable him to use his own skills and interests to the full. Efficient preparation and planning is required and here it is necessary to work within a basic framework to ensure that all the important points are covered. The amount of planning will depend on the situation; a teacher bringing a group into an area is going to have more planning to do than an instructor who collects his group at the start of the day. The visiting teacher, although faced with more planning, will have a possible advantage in that he should easily be able to bring a freshness into the situation which the instructor, knowing the area and the possible walks like the back of his hand, might find more difficult to achieve. It is quite difficult for some instructors to maintain an appearance of enthusiasm for a walk which has been repeated many times but it is important that one should seek to do so for a lack of enthusiasm is easily detectable and will quickly spread to the party. The compensation which the instructor has is his much greater knowledge of all the points of interest with which to enliven the day.

Although the visiting teacher may not have the working knowledge of an area which the permanent instructor will have it should go without saying that he must have a basic familiarity with the area and the proposed route and a level of expertise at least up to the standard of the Mountain Leadership Certificate. The teacher must have the full confidence of his party at all times and any lack of certainty will make itself felt just as quickly as any other emotion. The key to good work of any kind in the mountains is to have the right people in the right place at the right time with the right knowledge and the right equipment.

Pre-planning a Mountain Day

Certain factors must be taken into account when planning an outing and the following points apply equally to expeditions of several days' duration and to one-day sessions.

Permission for the proposed expedition must be obtained in the first instance from the headmaster. If he approves of the plan it is then necessary to obtain the permission of the Local Education Authority. Once the L.E.A. has given the go-ahead the parents of the children concerned must be contacted and their permission for the child to go obtained. They should be fully informed of what the expedition entails, the nature of the activities, the possible dangers and the qualifications of the staff before being asked to give their permission in writing.

Insurance: The L.E.A. should have insurance provision for outdoor activities if they form a regular part of the programme of some or all of the county schools. However it is necessary to find out exactly what the cover is and what regulations govern it. The basic requirements are third-party cover and personal accident cover for the staff and the group.

Transport needs to be arranged well in advance. The choice of transport needs to be governed by its suitability for the size of group, the amount of equipment and its cost. Times and meeting places should be arranged, and clear, written details given to the members of the party.

Cost: When the total cost has been estimated it should then be decided how this is going to be met. Possibly part or all of the cost may be met by a school or L.E.A. grant but it should be clear to all who is to pay for what and when the money has to be handed in.

Medical Considerations: All the party should be physically fit and for some expeditions it may be considered necessary to obtain medical certificates to this effect. It is important that the staff in charge should be aware of any members who suffer from anything which could prove dangerous, i.e. diabetes, epilepsy, asthma, etc. Provided that the condition is known the person need not necessarily be debarred from a particular activity, in fact it may even be beneficial, but if in doubt a medical opinion should be sought.

Contact: A system of contact between the group and home should be established so that messages can be passed either way. A lot of anxiety can be saved, for example, if it is possible to let parents know that the party has been delayed for some reason and on expeditions of more than one day, it is equally important that a member of the group can be contacted in the event of some misfortune occurring at home.

The above are all administrative points which largely affect the teacher who is bringing a party to the mountains rather than the instructor at a centre. One point from the above which should concern the instructor, however, is the question of insurance. He should take steps to find out exactly what cover he has under the terms of his employment and to supplement this if necessary.

The choice of route will depend upon the following factors.

Number in the Party: There is no correct number for a walking party as a variety of factors will influence the decision. Difficult routes are better done with small numbers as are long routes. As a general rule the larger a party the slower it will be. Guide-lines for numbers would be a minimum of four, so that in the event of an accident it would be possible to send down two people with a message while one stayed with the casualty, and a maximum of ten students to one member of staff.

Parties larger than this are cumbersome and hard to control and the more people involved the less enjoyable the situation and the less teaching can be done. The ideal number for the average walk would be six or seven students to one instructor. Seven is about the maximum number which one can check at a glance without having to resort to counting and this makes it much easier to ensure that all the group are together at any given time.

On walks which entail a considerable amount of scrambling it is sometimes preferable to have a larger group accompanied by two instructors. This enables full control to be maintained on each section of scrambling as one instructor can lead while the other is able to give help and advice to the group from the foot of the section.

Age and Ability: Different age groups will obviously have differing levels of stamina and will need to be catered for accordingly. Groups with proven ability will be able to undertake a greater range of expeditions than novices and care should be taken to ensure that previous walks are not repeated by checking on what has been done on former occasions.

Time of Year: The time of year will determine the hours of daylight and the likely weather conditions which will in turn influence the equipment requirements. Where possible it is best to organize walks so that most of the route is in the direction of the prevailing wind.

Equipment: If the children are expected to provide their own personal equipment it will be necessary to check the major items, i.e. boots, anoraks, overtrousers and rucksacks to ensure that they are up to the necessary standard. Those who have not got equipment will need advice on what to buy bearing in mind that beginners do not necessarily require the best or most expensive items but what they have should be strong, serviceable and suited to the purpose. Instructors and teachers need to have a wide range of experience of various types of equipment in order to be able to give sound advice. A great deal of equipment for outdoor activities can be made quite easily and this can provide useful links in the school situation between craft, domestic science/sewing and outdoor activity departments. There are many advantages in making equipment, the maker gets a sense of satisfaction out of using a piece of equipment which he has made himself and treats it with more care and respect than something hired or loaned. It usually costs far less to make than to buy and will often provide a stimulus to learn the necessary craft skills.

Clothing and equipment for mountaineering will be fully dealt with later but each member of the group should have adequate clothing and boots and a rucksack which should contain map, compass, whistle, spare clothes, food, emergency rations, torch and a polythene bivouac bag. A thermos containing a hot drink is a useful addition to the above at most times of the year. The party should also have the following communal items: a sleeping bag or duvet, 120 ft (36 m) of 9-mm rope, a comprehensive first aid kit, flares and a means of making a hot drink. For arduous expeditions at times of the year when bad weather is to be expected a lightweight tent should also be included. In some cases the leader may carry the communal equipment but usually it is good policy to allow the group to share the responsibility for their well-being by distributing it among them.

Time: The amount of time available for a walk will be governed by the number of daylight hours and the planned route should be such that it can be covered well within the limits. The standard formula for calculating the length of time of a walk is that of Naismith's Rule which allows one hour for every three miles walked plus half an hour for every thousand feet of ascent. Time must also be allowed for lunch and other breaks. Thus a walk of nine miles with a height gain of 3,000 ft would take four and a half hours steady walking so a time allowance of six hours should give ample opportunity for breaks and lunch.

When working on metric maps the nearest metric equivalent is four kilometres per hour plus half an hour for every 300 m of ascent.

Access: Make sure that the access to your proposed route is not restricted in any way and that the route does not involve crossing walls, fences or farmland.

Points of Interest: The more the better. Not only is the route going to be more interesting and enjoyable but they provide natural breaks.

Bad Weather Alternatives: These should always be planned as the weather could be totally unsuitable for the proposed route on the day. These are complete outings in themselves and should not be confused with escape routes.

Escape Routes: A walk should have one or more places where it is possible to abandon it easily and quickly should this become necessary due to bad weather or other emergencies.

Staff Experience: This is probably the most important single factor in determining a walk. Great demands are made upon them both to make the walk a success and to ensure that it is carried out in safety. Children in particular are very trusting and will put all their faith in the leader and are completely dependent upon his ability for their safety. The leader must be a competent mountaineer capable of moving easily over rough terrain and in scrambling situations. There are no short cuts to this and no substitutes for experience and sound judgement. Navigation must also be of a high standard. A leader who is hesitant in a difficult navigational situation or who fails to find his objective will quickly lose the confidence of his party.

Route Cards: These should be made out beforehand. These may be complex and detailed or quite simple depending upon the ability of the leader and his knowledge of the area. Generally speaking the less the leader knows about the area the more detailed his route card needs to be. A leader who knows an area well may only require a list of key bearings for certain points where another would require times for each leg, pacings, distances and a detailed description of the terrain for most of the route.

A route description should always be left at base with full details of bad weather alternatives and escape routes.

On the Day

i Obtain a weather report. A general report can be obtained from the radio and a comparison with a weather chart such as the one given in the *Guardian* daily should give an overall picture of the weather and its likely pattern during the day. For a detailed report on the area which you intend to visit, the nearest meteorological office or R.A.F. met. office will give a very accurate synopsis if contacted by telephone. Important points to note are whether the situation is improving or deteriorating and what the wind speed and direction is. Remember that conditions on the tops are going to be considerably harsher than the valleys, temperatures will drop and winds will be stronger.

ii Leave the route and party details with a responsible person at base. Allow plenty of leeway when giving an E.T.A. at base or transport, it is much better to be early than late.

iii Check individual and group equipment. Do not assume that because a party of children has been told what to bring they will actually bring it.

iv Before setting off see that individuals are not over- or under-dressed for the conditions, that their rucksacks are well packed and their bootlaces properly fastened.

v If transport is being used check that the pick-up time and place is known.

vi If they do not already know, show the group the proposed route on the map. The more they are involved in the day the more they are going to gain from it. They should be aware of where they are starting from, where they are going and how long it is likely to take.

Role of the Leader

The leader of the party must carry the responsibility for the enjoyment, training and safety of the group while on the hill and to be able to carry out these duties efficiently he must be able to make a good contact with the group. It is likely that the teacher with a party from his own school will have already established this contact, particularly if he has been out in an informal situation with them before. He also has an additional bonus in that there can be a great deal of feedback to his work in the classroom situation. The relaxed atmosphere of the mountain day allows both pupils and staff to see each other in a different light and inevitably leads to an improved relationship in the formal school situation.

The instructor has to make his contact quickly, he perhaps has only a week or even less to get to know the group and to project his own personality. He must gain the respect of the group for his ability and by the strength of his character and personality for in an emergency it is essential that he is obeyed without question. In parties of a similar age group it is not always the nominal leader who is the true leader of the party. It is very difficult to pin down the characteristics which determine good leadership but decisiveness is an important factor and it has often been the case that when an emergency has arisen and the nominal leader has shown indecision the true leader of the group has materialized in the person who has been prepared to make decisions and who has sufficient personality to have them accepted by the remainder. This situation should never arise in parties under training except on those occasions when unaccompanied walks or camps are being carried out, where it is an important factor to be taken into consideration. The leader must, by his actions, leave no doubt of his control and ability. A party of novices faced with a difficult situation, perhaps an error of route finding towards the end of a misty day on the tops, will quickly become demoralized if they feel that the leader, in whom they have placed their total trust, is not in complete charge of the situation. Confidence and sound judgement come from experience, there is no substitute. All who take parties on to the mountains must have a wealth of experience of many areas at all times of the year from which to draw and should have considerable familiarity with the area which is being used.

During a walk there are many practical details which have to be dealt with by the leader. His is the responsibility of ensuring that the necessary group equipment is assembled. In some circumstances he may choose to carry all this himself but usually he will distribute it around the group so that they feel that they are involved with the provisions for their own safety and are aware of what is being carried for them as a whole.

The leader has to judge and set a pace which is suited to the party. The aim should be to establish a pace and rhythm at the start of the walk which is still being held at the finish by all the members. Beginners

know nothing of the so-called walking skills and these are best introduced as the occasion arises rather than trotting out a list of facts at the
start. Many will move quite naturally over rough terrain without any
help whereas others may require considerable assistance at first. To be
able to give this assistance it is necessary for the teacher to be aware of
the reasons for his own effortless movement in places which novices find
difficult. He should be able to analyse his own movements if he is going
to be of any help to others. The tricks of the trade – rhythm, length of
stride and use of irregularities to keep the foot flat on steep ground –
should be passed on to those who show a need for them at any given
time.

A great deal can be learned about the balance and walking ability of
one's group by listening to the sounds which they make when following
over rough terrain and by observing their movement in a variety of
situations. Think what you can learn about them by sight and hearing,
are they talking or not, if not why? If they are talking what are they
saying and does it have any relevance to the situation? Does the noise
which their feet is making help you in any way? Do they look bored,
interested, worried, fatigued, absorbed in what they are doing? Do they
appear to be moving easily? Eyes and ears can tell you a lot about your
group in a very short time if you are able to interpret what you observe.

When you do offer help and advice remember that climbing terminology is very specialized and make sure that you use terms which they can
understand.

After passing obstacles such as short scrambling sections wait to see
that all are negotiating them safely. In some cases it is better to be at the
rear to offer help, point out footholds and so on particularly if there is a
good, safe gathering place at the top or end of the obstacle. The position
of the leader in the group will constantly be dictated by the situations
encountered. The front is the easiest place to be for much of the time but
it is by no means always the most desirable or best place. The optimum
position of the leader should always be decided by the needs of the party
at that time. If it is necessary to maintain the correct pace, perhaps in a
situation where navigation depends on good timing or pacing, then the
leader should be at the front but consider the following situations,
which are by no means exhaustive.

i A well defined footpath or track.

ii A grassy slope.

iii A mixed slope, small cliffs and grass.

iv Scrambling situations, easy and difficult.

v Scree slopes, ascent and descent.

vi A short, icy traverse crossing the bed of a gully.

vii Snow slopes, up down and across.

How would you position yourself in any of the given circumstances if you were (a) by yourself, (b) with another teacher in (c) good and bad weather conditions. Try to compare your answers with those of another experienced person. You will find that there is no one answer to many of them but can you satisfactorily justify your choice and can he do likewise? Again it becomes apparent that good judgement is required to arrive at the decision which is going to be of most value to the party.

Keeping the group together, particularly when it is of mixed ability is one of the most frequently encountered problems of walking. How should one deal with the inevitable straggler? Obviously the pace should be suited to the slower members of the group but the odd really slow one can often be encouraged a great deal by keeping him near the front, talking to him or, on easy ground, giving him some responsibility for choosing the route. These measures are most likely to be effective if he can be spotted as the weak link before it has become really apparent to himself and others. The appointment of a rear man needs some thought. It is easier with a known group than an unknown but it should be possible to organize the situation so that everyone in the party gets a go with the weaker ones being used on the easier stretches and the strong and reliable members rearguarding the trickier sections. In this way nobody feels left out or useless and no one person has to be continually at the back. It should be stressed at the beginning that the backman must not allow anyone to fall behind him and must also warn the leader if the party is beginning to straggle. The danger of backmen swopping over without being told to do so by the leader should also be explained.

One of the things which a leader has to decide is where and when rest stops need to be made. This will vary to a certain extent according to the party but a skilful leader will be able to incorporate rest stops into the walk without making them obvious by using them to point out things of interest. The lunch stop also requires some thought. The top of the mountain is not normally the best place as it usually offers maximum exposure to the weather, better is a sheltered spot *en route* and even better two or more short stops, particularly in winter. A little and often is a good maxim for eating on mountains.

Blisters can spoil a mountain day and perhaps a whole holiday so emphasis should be placed on trying to prevent them. Make sure that the party has well fitting socks, preferably without darns and well fitting, properly tied boots. It should be impressed upon them that the time to ask for a plaster is when the heel first starts to smart rather than when the blister has formed.

Awareness is the keynote to the role of the leader. He needs to be constantly aware of the changing situation as the day progresses, the points of potential danger, the mood and morale of the group, the weather, stragglers, the time factors and the possibilities of adding further items of enjoyment and interest to the walk.

Scrambling and Ropework

Scrambling is one of the ways in which a mountain day can be made more interesting and most parties of youngsters will prefer a route which takes in some scrambling to one which consists entirely of straight-forward walking. When scrambling is met for the first time it may be necessary to point out a few of the basic rules for moving on rock if none of the party is familiar with rock climbing techniques. The most important points which should be brought out are the need to test all the holds, particularly important in the scrambling situation where a greater number of loose holds is likely to be found than on a well used rock face, three-point contact, an upright stance and the need to be careful about knocking down loose rock on to other members of the group especially from the top of the scrambling section.

It may be necessary to use the rope to safeguard the odd person on the very occasional bit of scrambling but on a mountain walk the rope should be regarded as part of the emergency equipment rather than the walk being planned around the use of the rope. If the rope has to be used to safeguard the whole of the party it is usually because the route has been badly planned or things have gone wrong. The techniques of rope handling for such situations have been dealt with in Chapter 1 and are also fully covered from the mountain walking aspect in the *Mountain Leadership* handbook (see Bibliography). The latter emphasizes the use of the rope only but people with a rock climbing background will find it useful to carry a couple of karabiners and slings, the use of which can make the ropework in an emergency situation swifter and less complex. A point which is little appreciated about the use of fixed handlines to safeguard difficult places is that not only are they time-consuming to rig but, unless another rope is used as a safety rope, the instructor has no control over the pupil but relies entirely on his ability to hold on to

1. *The End Tie.* Note that the free end of the figure eight knot has been tucked back into the knot. This is a satisfactory and less cumbersome alternative to securing the end with a hitch around the rope.

2. *The Spike Anchor.*

a. The rope tied back into the waistbelt. With only the slight tension of leaning on the belay ropes the belt is pulled away from the body and consequently the live rope around the waist does not bear on the static ropes of the anchor system.

b. The rope tied back into the karabiner in the traditional way. This can become unwieldy when the climber is attached to more than one anchor.

3. Belaying to a thread anchor using a sling and karabiner.

4a. Belaying to a thread anchor using the rope alone.

b. A detailed view of how the ropes are tied back to the waist.

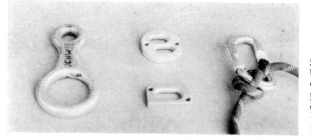

5. *Friction Devices.* Left to right: figure eight descendeur, Sticht plates for use with 9 mm double rope and 11 mm single rope, Italian hitch.

6. A useful small crag providing a variety of situations and problems for basic work. It has a good top with a variety of anchors, an easy way down and a broad, flat base.

7. Hand jam.

8. *The Plas y Brenin Weight Drop Machine.* The concrete block weighs 10 st (63·5 kg), is raised by the ratchet winch at the foot and released by a pull on the thin cord. A fall on to a runner can be simulated as shown, or with the student belayed on the platform to the right of the block, a free leader fall or falling second situation may be arranged.

9. *Prusiking.*

a. From a relaxed position in the sit-sling the climber can use both hands to slide up the foot sling.

b. The higher the leg is raised the greater the height gained in one sequence of movements. Turning the knee outward facilitates a greater lift of the leg.

c. As he stands up straight the climber moves his waist prusik up and then relaxes into his sit-sling. A combination of Jumar and Klemheist knot is shown here but any prusik-type knot or device may be used. Knots are more difficult to use but are satisfactory over short distances. In situations where long ascents have to be made it is normal to use mechanical prusiking devices and some climbers like to have a chest loop attached to the top prusiker to give extra support.

10. In this comparison of new and old rope the flattening of the lay and the general fuzziness of outline caused by severing of the outer fibres can be clearly seen.

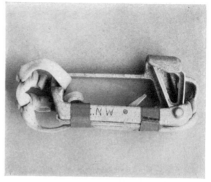

12. A Jumar clamp which has had its strong points linked with tape. In use the attachment is to both the tape loops at the base.

11. The U.I.A.A. symbol.

13. *The Thomas Stretcher.* This model is fitted with a plastic-covered wire bed and the strong points have been permanently linked with rope to facilitate lowering. The near handles are shown in the retracted position.

14a. *The MacInnes Stretcher.* The carrying straps have been omitted for clarity. Note the built-in alloy headguard. This model is fitted with a nylon mesh bed.

b. The MacInnes Stretcher folded for carrying.

15. *The Mariner Stretcher.* Note the wheel and leg splint. The rear man is carrying the steel lowering cable used on cliff rescues.

16a. The Tragsitz.

b. In use most of the patient's weight is taken on the lowering rope.

17. The three-quarter prone position.

18. Ice axe braking, basic arrest position. Note that the body is arched to put pressure on the pick (not possible to do when wearing crampons), and that the lower hand covers the spike.

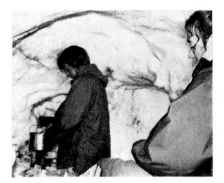

20. Snowholing can be fun.

19. Start of a forward roll. The axe is inevitably close to the face and care needs to be taken to avoid injury when practising.

21. Tents are highly inflammable.

22. Two types of pack-frame in use. The right-hand one has a home-made sack.

23. Mountain tent.

24. A water pipe can provide opportunity for adventure.

25. Sea-level traversing reveals a variety of adventure situations but needs careful and expert supervision. Note that the weak swimmers have been equipped with buoyancy aids.

the handline. For this reason it is invariably better to use the rope as a direct safeguard, tying the party on one at a time and protecting them while they climb down or even lowering them. Similarly the party should never move together when roped in situations where a fall by one member could dislodge the whole party and jeopardize their safety. Horizontal ridges are particularly dangerous and it requires great skill for even a small party of competent mountaineers to be able to move together in safety when roped. This technique is permissible in open terrain, where there is no danger of a fall, to link the party in white-out conditions or in high winds, which can be very frightening for youngsters as they are so much more easily blown off their feet than adults.

Mountain Hazards

Many accidents to walking parties are due to a lack of knowledge of the potential dangers inherent in any mountain area. Some of our mountain areas are more dangerous than others at certain times of the year. Scotland in winter, for example, can have weather which is Arctic in severity and which will tax the survival ability of the strongest and best-equipped parties, but all mountain areas can have dangerous conditions, situations and combinations of circumstances for which the hill walker must go prepared.

Wind: The warmth offered by clothing is due largely to its ability to trap a layer of still air close to the body. This air layer being a poor conductor will insulate the body against loss of heat. If the air layer is disturbed in any way heat is lost. Wind disturbs the air layer in two ways: firstly, by causing the clothing to flap, it sets up a bellows action which tends to expel the warm, still air and suck in cold air; secondly, if an outer layer of windproof clothing is not worn, the wind will penetrate the clothing whisking away the warm air. A third factor which influences the trapped air layer is that of convection within the garments. Warm air, being lighter than cold, rises, cools and descends setting up convection currents. This is often noticeable in cold conditions as a draught down the neck.

Winds blow more fiercely on exposed mountain-tops and ridges where there are no natural windbreaks and also in gullies and on cols which tend to funnel the wind. Even with the best and most adequate of clothing wind can prove to be a major hazard in mountaineering and has

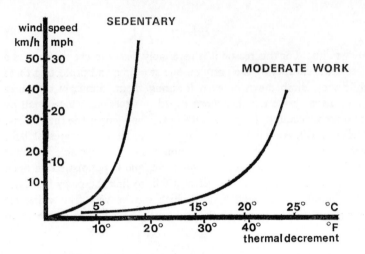

FIG. 6. The thermal wind decrement to be subtracted from the shade temperature to give equivalent still air temperature. Note that it depends on the amount of work being done. (J. M. Adam, *Exploration Medicine*, John Wright and Sons Ltd.)

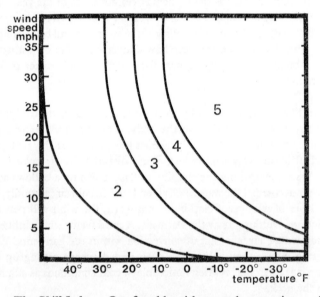

FIG. 7. *The Chill Index.* 1 Comfortable with normal precautions. 2 Very cold, travel becomes uncomfortable on overcast days. 3 Bitterly cold, travel is uncomfortable on clear, sunny days. 4 Freezing of flesh begins according to degree of activity. 5 Survival efforts are required.

contributed to many mountaineering accidents. Garments should be designed to reduce the heat losses described by being close fitting to reduce the bellows effect without being unduly constricting, windproof and, to minimize loss by convection, close fitting at neck and wrists. Despite all precautionary measures heat loss will still be increased by wind and will also be determined by the amount of work being done (Fig. 6). The effect of the wind is thus an apparent reduction of the still air temperature. A walker on a cold day in calm conditions might feel quite comfortable but as the wind strength increases he becomes steadily colder although the still air temperature may not have altered at all. Fig. 7 gives an indication of the zones determined by temperature and wind although it should be noted that these zones are influenced greatly by other factors, the amount of work being done (Fig. 6) and the humidity playing important roles.

Rain: The danger from rain is that it encourages heat loss from the body by conduction. Water is a good conductor unlike the air around the body and the materials of the clothing which retains it. If the clothing is allowed to become wet either from rain or from condensation inside the garments much of its insulating value will be lost. Mountain areas in the British Isles do tend to have a great deal of rain, the average annual rainfall on the top of Snowdon, for example, being in the region of 200 in (508 cm) while that of the coastal area only a few miles away is around 34 in (86 cm). Obviously rain must be taken into account when considering suitable clothing. Wet cold conditions are those most likely to lead to exposure. The increased conductivity of the garments combines with the effects of the wind, drastically lowering the body temperature.

A further hazard of rain is that it makes every rock and boulder slippery and grassy slopes, too, can become potentially dangerous, particularly to those clad in waterproof suits which have a smooth, plastic outer surface. Such garments have very low frictional properties in the wet and a fall on an apparently innocuous slope can be very difficult to control. Driving rain reduces visibility and increases the problems of navigation, and it is well to verify the strength of the party and what is hoped to be gained before venturing on to the tops in wet gale conditions.

Temperature: As we have seen, temperature and wind are interrelated with regard to bodily warmth but temperature will also affect the terrain quite considerably. If the valley temperature is a little above freezing the temperature at 3,000 ft (914 m) will be below freezing due to the lapse rate, which is between 35·3° and 37·4° F (2° and 3° C) according to conditions. The temperature drop will be greatest on clear, dry days and least on those which are humid with a thick cloud cover. Thus we can expect to find frost or ice-glazed rock and snow in the higher reaches of the mountains on many occasions when conditions in the valleys are above freezing.

Convex Slopes: These present a danger when they are snow covered or when grassy and wet. Once a slide has commenced it becomes increasingly difficult to stop as the slope becomes steeper the further one slides.

Poor Visibility: In addition to driving rain poor visibility can be due to mist or white-out conditions. It is important to keep the party together and to keep a careful check on the route in these conditions. Good navigation is essential here and an effort should be made to verify the position of the party at every opportunity. In white-out conditions in particular, it is very easy to go wildly astray in a very short space of time.

River Crossings: Nearly every mountaineer is faced with a potentially hazardous river crossing at some time. The more remote the area the less likely the chance that there will be bridges across the rivers. Unless they are in spate mountain rivers do not normally present serious problems but when faced with a difficult crossing the golden rule is not to attempt it unless it is essential that you do so. A walk of several miles to the nearest bridge is preferable to drowning and if there is no bridge it may be necessary to wait until the flood subsides. Mountain rivers flood quickly and go down quickly and rivers fed by glacier melt-water will be forded more easily in the dawn than the late afternoon. If, after careful consideration, a decision is made to cross, a rope should be used as a safeguard. Leaders should familiarize themselves with methods of using the rope effectively and the best places at which to make crossings.

Lightning: This is common enough on the mountains to constitute a hazard and party leaders should be aware of the likely paths of ground currents and the safest places in which to sit out an electrical storm.

Benightment: This is often due to bad navigation and/or poor planning or it can be due to a combination of several of the previously mentioned weather conditions. If a route-finding error leads into difficult or hazardous terrain it is usually better to retreat and find the correct route than to try to press on even if this entails further ascent. Many parties who spend an involuntary night out do so because of an unwillingness to admit that they are in the wrong place and a determination to press on to try and regain easy ground.

If benightment is inevitable try to keep up the morale of the party and find a place to stop before it gets dark. The aim should be to get as low as possible on a lee slope and obtain whatever shelter is available, building windbreaks if necessary. The leader should ensure that all members of the party are made as comfortable as possible, that they all have some food, put on their reserve clothing and change gloves and socks if these are wet. Any insulation in the form of bracken etc. should be utilized to put beneath the polythene bags and the group should be instructed to take off their boots and put their feet into their rucksacks for warmth. If there is any likelihood of frost the boots must also go into the rucksacks to avoid freezing overnight.

Clothing and Equipment for General Mountaineering

The following notes are intended as a guide to the principles underlying the type of clothing and equipment which we use in the mountains for those teachers who wish to equip their parties adequately while conforming to a budget. Nowadays there is a tremendous range of equipment available and it does not necessarily follow that the most expensive is going to be the best. Before purchasing any item of equipment the teacher should decide how much he is prepared to pay, what use will be made of the equipment, who is to use it, whether it can be improvised or made satisfactorily and whether it is worth while to do so. The clothing of each member of a party under instruction should be adequate for the particular activity but that of the leader should be more than adequate and he should carry ample spare clothing to be able to deal with an emergency in which he may be called upon to take care of other people as well as himself.

Man is a tropical animal and cannot live comfortably in temperatures below 68°F (20°C) without clothing. His body temperature has to be maintained within quite narrow limits and both excessively high and

low body temperatures will quickly lead to death. Although heat-stroke
and heat-exhaustion cannot be discounted they are easily controlled in
the mountain environment by adjusting the clothing as necessary. Our
main concern is usually to prevent the body heat escaping which it can
do in four ways: convection, evaporation, radiation and conduction.
We have already seen how heat may be lost as a result of convection in
wind and by hot air rising from the clothing.

Evaporation is the conversion of a liquid to a vapour and in the case
of water considerable quantities of heat are required to achieve this. At
rest the body loses 0·9 of a pint (or half a litre) of water through the skin
each day and a quarter of the body heat produced during that period is
required to evaporate it. In cold conditions the vapour can recondense
on to the clothing and then again evaporate slowly causing further heat
loss. For many years waterproof outer clothing was considered to be
unsuitable for mountaineering because of the resultant condensation
and a great deal of research was devoted to developing a material which
would be water- and windproof but also vapour permeable. However,
although materials have been developed which come very close to the
ideal, the fact that saturated garments are going to cause greater heat
losses by conduction and evaporation than those made damp by condensation has caused opinion to swing in favour of completely waterproof lightweight outer garments. These are usually plastic, plastic on a
material backing, which is stronger, or nylon with a waterproof backing.
Often the latter does not retain its waterproof qualities for so long as a
plastic garment but has a less slippery outer surface which makes it a
safer proposition for winter use.

It has been noted that water is a good conductor and that heat will be
lost if the garments are allowed to become wet. Further losses by conduction occur through contact with the cold ground and by touching and
handling cold objects though these losses are kept at a minimum by the
insulation of rubber-soled boots and dry gloves.

Radiation can be the source of both heat gains and losses. Radiant heat
is gained from the sun and from the reflective surface of snow and in the
absence of sun the body will lose heat by radiation to colder surroundings.

It will be seen that suitable clothing has to contend with temperature,
wind and moisture. In addition it must not be too bulky or it will inter-
fere with movement, it should fit well, be durable and it is advantageous,
for reasons of safety, to have brightly coloured garments. In situations
where the predominant factor is going to be dry-cold, vapour per-

meability is important otherwise water vapour from body losses will re-condense as ice on the outer garments.

Effective temperature control is best achieved by layers of clothing. The layers trap more air and help to resist convection. They also allow for quick temperature control and adjustment as the environmental conditions vary. Synthetic pile materials have largely superseded the traditional string vest both on the grounds of comfort and efficiency but these tend to be expensive. There is still a place for the cheap, cellular vest as the base garment of the layer although some people prefer wool next to their skins. The main advantage of wool is that it does not lose all its properties of insulation when wet as it is still able to trap air within its fibres but many people find it too irritating to have next to the skin. Subsequent layers should be made up of garments composed of materials which trap air readily, woollen shirts and sweaters being the commonest garments used on the upper body for this purpose.

For warmth the more layers the better but one should try to ensure that they are graded in size so that constriction and bulk are kept to a minimum. Fastenings should be such that some of the garments can be opened at the neck and wrists to increase ventilation quickly and easily when necessary. Light garments should be used wherever possible to keep down the total weight of clothing worn.

Wind and moisture problems are mainly countered by the outer layer of clothing which will be discussed later. If we now consider the parts of the body in detail we can see how the above principles guide our choice of clothing.

The Head If the rest of the body is adequately clothed a considerable proportion of the heat lost can be through the head and face if they are not also protected. A figure of 40 per cent of the total heat loss has been cited in this context and although high this does not seem improbable. The blood supply to the head is copious and, unlike the other extremities, cannot be reduced in cold conditions. It is therefore extremely important to provide adequate protection for the head and face as with-out it the blood circulating in the head is rapidly cooled and will, in turn, lower the temperature of the inner core and vital organs of the body.

Any woollen hat will give reasonable warmth and it is not necessary to insist that children obtain any specialized headgear for occasional moun-tain walking in the summertime. The standard mountaineering head-gear is the brushed wool balaclava or 'Jaeger' obtainable from almost

any mountaineering equipment supplier at a reasonable price. Its greatest asset is its versatility. It can be worn as a bobcap, pulled down to
cover the ears or fully extended to cover the whole of the head and most
of the face and tucked into the neck of the sweater to eliminate draughts
and cut warm air losses. The fact that it is made of brushed wool adds to
its thickness and increases insulation.

The Upper Body The first layer should be a ventilating layer to increase air space and allow perspiration to evaporate freely. A cellular
vest will do this adequately but an ordinary vest may also be considered
satisfactory at most times of the year. Woollen shirts are popular among
climbers as a second layer because of the ease of varying the ventilation
and also because a woven material tends to be more windproof than a
knitted one. Shirts of this type tend to be expensive and if one is to be
purchased specially one should ensure that it is long in the tail to prevent
it working out of the trousers. A long tail can also be most useful when
repairs have to be made and patches from this can prolong the life of the
garment considerably!

Over the shirt two or more layers of woollen sweaters, according to
conditions, will give adequate warmth and versatility. Any old sweaters
will do but preferably they should be light and close knitted rather than
thick, open knit which is less windproof and does not trap the air so well.
Traditionally Shetland and Kashmir wools are the best but these are
expensive.

A highly efficient modern alternative to wool is the 'polar suit' of
artificial fibre pile. Designed originally for use by Norwegian sailors in
Arctic waters these garments are warm, light, well fitting, durable, quick
drying and easily ventilated. They are expensive but a worthwhile
investment for the committed mountaineer.

The Hands It is very important to protect the hands adequately. They
are the part of the body most likely to be affected first by frostbite, if
exposed, as the supply of blood to the extremities is automatically
reduced by the body in cold conditions. In winter at least one spare pair
of gloves should be carried in addition to the ones normally in use.

Mittens are generally warmer than gloves and quite suitable for
mountain walking where fine use of the fingers is seldom going to be
necessary. The best material for warmth is wool and Dachstein mitts
made of felted wool are very popular. They remain quite efficient even
when wet being made of pre-shrunk, oiled wool which is windproof,

showerproof and snowproof. All mittens and gloves for mountain use should have a long gauntlet to provide protection for the wrist where the radial artery runs close to the surface creating an area of high heat loss.

In situations where it is occasionally necessary to use the fingers, e.g. when fitting crampons, a fine pair of silk inner gloves is useful in cutting down some of the heat loss which occurs when handling cold objects.

In situations where a fine touch is necessary, such as rock climbing, fingerless mittens may be used in cold conditions but in extreme conditions where full protection is required the best thing is a well-fitting ski glove.

The grip of any woollen glove can be improved by sewing a piece of thin, supple leather on to the palm. This will also help to prolong its life.

The Legs Jeans are not suitable wear for the hills. They are not warm or windproof and give no insulation when wet. This should be stressed to children preparing for an expedition, as they are so popular for casual wear.

Breeches and knee-length stockings are most popular with mountaineers because they allow more freedom of movement and avoid flapping material around the lower legs. They should have ample room in the seat and an efficient method of fastening below the knee. Most breeches tend to be made of heavy, fairly windproof material and are not normally worn with another layer underneath except in very cold conditions when long johns or polar trousers may be worn.

Novices will be adequately protected in flannel trousers throughout the summer months but early or late in the year should wear long johns underneath or flannel pyjamas as a good alternative. An old pair of trousers can very easily be converted to knee breeches by cutting off the legs about mid-calf, tapering the ends and putting in a draw-cord to tie below the knee and using the cut off legs to patch any weak areas.

Socks should be woollen, free from darns and thick. Most children and parents have no idea what is meant by a thick sock so this needs careful explanation if they are to arrive adequately equipped. The best specialist socks and stockings available at present are loopstitch construction. They are comfortable to wear, warm, durable and the stockings have elasticated tops which obviates the necessity to have the breeches tightly fastened below the knee, often the cause of circulation problems in the past.

The question of whether one should wear one or two pairs of socks has long been a bone of contention among mountaineers. With modern, well-padded boots one pair of socks will give the required warmth and comfort with the added advantages of greater sensitivity and a closer-fitting boot for rock climbing. The total outlay in socks is also only half the cost! When the consideration is purely that of walking a little extra padding and shock absorbency is certainly afforded by two pairs of socks and I would always recommend two pairs if the boots are to be hired. Hire boots cannot be expected to be a perfect fit, all boots take time to adjust to the shape of the foot, and an extra sock will go a long way towards ironing out the individual differences.

When buying boots my advice would always be to buy them to fit comfortably with only one pair of thick socks. Any subsequent stretch can then be dealt with by wearing a second pair of socks if necessary.

Boots Boots are essential for people venturing into rough and moun-tainous country even for fairly low-level fieldwork. They give far greater ankle support than shoes and it is just as easy to sprain an ankle on a field trip to Cwm Idwal as it is to do so on the top of the Glyders.

You are accepting completely unnecessary responsibility if you agree to take people into the mountains in shoes, however strong, and are well within your rights to refuse to do so. Working boots such as Tuf boots, while better than shoes, are also not suitable for mountain use. The soles, although highly resistant to grease and the conditions of the factory floor, are not suited to mountain terrain and do not afford a sure grip on rock.

A good pair of boots is a very expensive item. Many of the features found in boots of this type are not necessary for mountain walking and some even hinder it so some thought must be given to the main purpose for which the boot will be used and the weather conditions which are likely to be encountered. Other factors governing choice will be who is going to use them, children or adults and whether they will be per-sonal or communal equipment. Having decided on requirements it is worth paying as much as you can afford for the particular type you have in mind. Boots are a very important item of equipment and it pays to have as good a quality as possible.

It is unreasonable to expect children to purchase a pair of boots on the strength of one mountain walk but it is also untenable to take them on to the hills without boots. This is the dilemma which often faces teachers. Some children will have their own boots and for the others there are two main possibilities: the school may decide to hold a small pool of com-munal boots if funds permit (parent/teacher associations may often raise funds for purposes of this kind) or it may be possible to hire boots in the area to which the party is going. In the latter case it is important to make an advance booking giving sizes as accurately as possible to avoid disappointment or delay on the day.

When fitting boots, new or hired, the following points will be found useful.

i Always try on new boots wearing the socks which you intend to use in them.

ii Fasten them up tightly and walk around the shop in them, leave them on for at least five minutes.

iii Boots should fit snugly, grip the heel and fit well around the instep when laced up. Heel movement is likely to cause blisters.

iv Toes should not touch the end of the boot. It is a mistake to assume that a boot will stretch; this varies enormously with the type of leather used and generally speaking a good-quality boot will stretch very little.

When comparing the merits of two or more makes of boot the following features are the ones which should influence your choice.

i The less seams there are the better. The boot will be more waterproof and less likely to fall apart with hard usage. Best-quality boots are made from one piece of leather joined at the heel.

ii A sewn-in tongue is necessary to keep out water when stepping into puddles, etc.

iii A boot which laces down to the toe is much easier to put on and take off.

iv Nearly all reasonable-quality boots now have 'D' rings or hooks rather than eyelets for lacing. A combination of the two with the 'D' rings in the lower half is common and popular.

v Good padding around the foot and ankle adds greatly to the comfort of the boot and gives additional insulation for winter use.

vi Walking boots should have a slight curve along the length of the sole and should be reasonably flexible. They should be broader fitting, for comfort, than a climbing boot and give good ankle support. There is no necessity to put children into heavy boots for summer walking, there are several good, reasonably priced makes of lightweight boot on the market which are perfectly adequate and will give the required support without the weary burden of a heavy weight on a young foot unused to wearing boots.

vii Climbing boots should have flat, rigid soles. This is usually achieved by the insertion of a metal plate into the inner sole. The whole boot should be narrower than a walking boot and the toe should be reasonably pointed to enable it to be inserted into cracks. The welt should be as narrow as possible to keep the weight of the body directly over small holds. Modern boots tend to have very high ankles, a feature not universally appreciated as some climbers like to have more ankle flexibility on rock than when walking. This type of boot is not designed for summer walking, the rigid sole inhibits the natural rolling action of the foot and the toe and heel are quickly worn down. A lot of money is wasted on climbing boots by people whose requirements would be better served by a good, stout walking boot.

viii The sole of the boot should not provide any problems if the purchase is made from a recognized mountaineering equipment supplier. All proper walking and climbing boots now have moulded rubber soles giving a good grip in most conditions other than very greasy, wet, lichenous rock and hard snow and ice. The major makes of sole are 'Vibram' and 'Itshide'. Very light, cheap boots with crêpe-type soles with little tread should be avoided. They are not very durable and are in the main, unsuitable for serious work.

Boots should be looked after carefully if they are to give good service. They should never be dried in direct heat but are better stuffed with dry newspaper and left in a warm, airy atmosphere. 'Drypacks' of silica gel are better than newspaper for extracting moisture and can be dried and used again indefinitely. The best treatment for the upper is ordinary wax boot polish worked well in with a rag (particularly around the welt) and then polished with a soft brush. The more coats which can be applied while the leather is dry the better the protection but at least twelve hours should be allowed between coats to let each layer harden. Oils and dubbin tend to soften the leather and some brands rot the stitching. Other than ordinary polish the only treatment which is beneficial is the occasional coat of Kiwi 'Wet-Prufe'.

Communal boots should have all mud and stones cleaned out of the cleats in the soles and should be washed to remove all mud from the uppers before being dried, polished and stored preferably on a boot rack in a dry, airy place. Washing also helps to remove the peat acid which, if allowed to remain, rots the stitching.

Outer Clothing To meet the exacting requirements imposed by the mountain environment the outer garments should be made of a material which is windproof, waterproof, heatproof, light, warm, vapour permeable, durable, colourful and cheap! Unfortunately, despite considerable research, this ideal material has not yet been discovered. It is easy enough to find materials which are wind- and waterproof but they often lack other desirable properties, particularly vapour permeability, and consequently tend to suffer from condensation problems. However in a predominantly wet-cold climate this type of outer garment is the most suitable. With good ventilation the condensation can be kept to within reasonable limits and there is no doubt in the minds of most experienced users that it is better to come back from a wet day slightly damp from condensation than absolutely saturated by rain and looking like a drowned rat.

The choice in waterproof garments lies between plastic or plastic-coated garments and proofed nylon garments. The former are the more permanently waterproof but tend to be rather stiff in cold weather. They are also more slippery than the nylon which can make them rather a liability in some conditions and the plastic tends to strip off when abseiling. The waterproof qualities of the proofed nylons depend on the type of proofing and the effectiveness of the seam sealing. Polyurethane proofing has a tendency to strip away from the nylon fairly quickly but more recently some nylons have been proofed with neo-prene which appears to be very much more durable. As with plastics, nylon has a low melting point and care needs to be taken when abseiling to avoid melting the material.

For use in dry-cold conditions where vapour permeability is import-ant Ventile, a natural fibre material, is highly satisfactory. Ventile is a finely woven material with interlocking fibres coming from the main threads. It is windproof, fairly waterproof, vapour permeable, durable, reasonably light in weight and will stand up to abseiling and other climbing abuses. It is, however, costly. A double thickness Ventile anorak can cost twice the amount one would pay for a plastic one. Ideally one should have at least two anoraks as no one anorak will meet all the requirements but if the budget restricts the choice to one it is better to go for one of the 100 per cent waterproof garments. Choice between nylon and plastic is largely a matter of personal preference. Another alternative, useful if climbing and abseiling are going to feature fairly frequently in the programme is to buy a cheap, showerproof, natural-fibre anorak and a lightweight proofed nylon anorak to slip over or under it in really wet weather.

When purchasing an anorak one should look for the following design features.

i *Size:* It should be large enough to take several layers of clothing underneath without being too large, cumbersome and draughty.

ii It should be long enough to cover the seat and thighs, particularly if waterproof.

iii Sleeves should not be too narrow and should have a draught seal at the cuffs. Care should be taken to ensure that this is not too tight or circulation to the hands may be impaired.

iv Many hoods are too small. The hood should be designed to pull round and almost enclose the face while still allowing free movement of the head. This means that the length of the hood from the nape of the neck to the top of the head must be adequate. Some hoods have a visor with an enclosed piece of copper wire round the edge. This can be bent to hold the hood in any position to act as a windbreak and is very useful in blizzard conditions. If not fitted on an otherwise serviceable anorak an extra strip of material incorporating a wire can easily be attached.

v Anoraks should have at least one large pocket, big enough to hold maps of the area. Most frequently this is a pouch pocket on the front of the anorak. It should have an efficient method of sealing and should preferably be waterproof. A tiny eyelet hole in one of the lower corners is useful to let out any water which gets in.

vi Methods of fastening: It should be possible to decrease as well as increase ventilation and anoraks should have a cord around the waist or lower edge so that draughts can be excluded.

vii The brighter the colour the easier it is to be seen. Often this is advantageous in difficult conditions or in case of accident.

Overtrousers are virtually a necessity when using waterproof anoraks as the water is not absorbed but runs straight down on to the thighs. The remarks regarding materials apply equally to overtrousers as to anoraks. A good pair of overtrousers should have zips at the ankles to facilitate getting them on and off over boots, and it should be possible to get at the trouser pockets without having to take the overtrousers down. If they are also going to be used for skiing it is worth having a pair with full-length zips which can be put on without having to remove the skis.

Gaiters fitting over the boot and extending to just below the knee are very useful in winter, especially when walking in breakable crust or deep snow. They are also useful in wet conditions and considerably increase the possibility of the feet remaining dry. The best ones are fully zipped down the back, making them easy to get on and off, and are made of canvas. Gaiters can also be made of waterproof nylon. These are lighter, slightly less expensive to buy and much easier to make than canvas ones but they tear more easily, particularly when used with crampons.

A useful supplementary item of clothing to carry in the rucksack is a woollen scarf to seal the air gap around the neck in very cold, windy, or wet conditions.

No mention has so far been made of down clothing which is with little doubt the finest form of insulating clothing, provided that it is kept dry. Down clothing is extremely light and obviates the need for layering provided that it is covered by a windproof outer. It is, however, very expensive and is now difficult to obtain. Best quality eiderdown is even more expensive and virtually unobtainable. A down jacket is beyond the pocket, range and requirements of the novice but it is a very useful item of equipment for the leader of a party. Being light and compact it forms an ideal reserve garment to carry in the rucksack in case of emergency.

Cheaper duvets containing down/feather mixtures or artificial fibres such as terylene batt and dacron are available but none as yet have the insulation properties of pure down and all are more bulky.

Improvisation At first sight the cost of fitting out a group of children with equipment for a mountain walk would appear to be prohibitive, nor is it realistic to imagine that they will be able to provide their own. Very few people, even enthusiasts, would contemplate kitting themselves out completely at any one time, and equipment tends to accumulate over the years. The school group will often find that the L.E.A. has a pool of camping and climbing equipment which can be hired. Unless this equipment has someone directly responsible for it the biggest problem lies in trying to ensure that the borrowers treat it with respect and return it in as good a condition as when it was received. A lot of good and expensive equipment is ruined in equipment pools because it is no one's responsibility, and it is up to the teachers concerned to see that hired equipment is treated with greater care than their own.

Very little personal equipment is normally available in L.E.A. pools but with a little care and patience most of it can be made or improvised. Anoraks, overtrousers, gaiters and rucksacks can be made at a fraction of the cost of bought articles and will be every bit as good if carefully made. Breeches, as we have seen, can be made from old trousers and very satisfactory mittens can be made from old socks or the sleeves of old sweaters. The only item which really has to be bought at first is boots and these, too, can occasionally be hired.

Chapter Six

Winter Mountaineering

Each winter brings with it a crop of accidents which frequently take place when the mountains are in true winter condition, i.e. when there is good consolidated snow cover. The important point about the majority of these accidents is that they occur on easy slopes to inexperienced climbers and walkers who have ventured out not knowing the most elementary things about winter conditions. As in the case of rock climbing, accidents to experienced parties attempting serious climbs are comparatively few. A most unfortunate aspect of winter accidents is that the falls which occur in these conditions tend to be long and uncontrolled, often leading to serious injury or death.

Undoubtedly this is a time of the year when any leader responsible for taking groups of young people into the hills will feel that his responsibilities weigh very heavily upon him. In snow conditions most of the normal, summer walking situations become inherently dangerous. One must cross and ascend snow slopes and yet no matter how easy these slopes may be, a slip, which could lead to a nasty fall, cannot be guarded against completely. Obviously one could rope up the party at a particularly difficult section but this cannot be done for the whole walk. One example will suffice to outline the problem in practical terms: the final few hundred feet of the Watkin path on Snowdon above Bwlch y Saethau is a weary scree slope in summer. In winter it can be transformed into a beautiful snow slope, fairly steep but not prohibitively so and one can kick or cut a line of bucket steps along the route of the path to the ridge but there is no guarantee that one of the party will not slip out of these steps. Should this occur it can result in a fall of over 1,000 ft (305 m) on mixed terrain and in fact this part of the mountain has claimed several victims. What is the answer? Does the party turn back, not go at all, or press on taking all reasonable precautions? In fact the Watkin path, when in winter condition, is probably the most dangerous of the common summer footpaths up Snowdon and is best avoided by complete novices but the same remarks apply to many other easy routes up British mountains. It is significant that the easiest of all ways up Snowdon, the railway track, claims more than its fair share of fatalities every hard winter.

Mountaineering is a high-risk sport and the art of good mountaineering lies in being able to assess the risks correctly, equate them with your own skill and competence and that of the party, and act accordingly. In winter one must be prepared to accept an increased degree of risk in the training situation or not do it at all. There are no other options. Careful training in the basic winter techniques will help to minimize this risk but cannot ensure that a novice will do the correct thing should he accidentally slip. Some authorities may feel that winter mountaineering has no place in the programme if absolute safety cannot be guaranteed but this is morally indefensible if the aim is to train mountaineers. It comes into the same category as the refusal to train leaders: 'Go away and try it yourself, come back if you survive.' If we undertake to train people as mountaineers I feel that we must be prepared to shoulder the risks inherent in dealing with some aspects of their training. If, on the other hand, the aim is to give children a number of new experiences and stimuli the situation is different and other conclusions may be drawn.

If winter training is to be given, the competence of staff taking parties on to the hills must be beyond all doubt. The teacher must have considerable personal winter experience and should be able to move with ease and familiarity on snow and ice. Awareness and mastery are the keywords. As in rock climbing the leader cannot afford to be but one step ahead of his pupils as here, more than in any other aspect, he may be called upon to produce great reserves of skill, stamina and expertise to ensure the safety of his party.

The primary task is to educate the novice in the basic essentials of movement in the mountains in winter so that he may safely attempt mountain walks in winter conditions. A certain amount of theory is essential and, because of the severity of winter weather, this is best carried out indoors. The level of attention is not likely to be very high if the group is cold and miserable.

The first and most important fact is the one which seems obvious to the experienced mountaineer but which is just not realized at all by the layman or novice. This is that snow on mountains is often quite hard and sometimes so hard that when kicked no impression is left by the boot. When snow such as this is encountered, even lying at quite a shallow angle, steps have to be cut in order to cross or ascend safely. This condition is often found in the spring when the mountains appear to be almost bare of snow and the inexperienced walker is lulled into a false sense of security. However, such snow as there is lies in the gullies and shady places on the north-facing slopes and is old and hard. The walker attempting to cross such a gully only a few yards wide may slip and perhaps find to his cost that although only narrow the gully is very long. It is obvious therefore that an ice axe must be carried, even if nothing more than an easy walk is contemplated and there appears to be little snow. Easy walks have a habit of suddenly becoming difficult and dangerous to those caught unprepared in wintertime.

The students need to see and handle a variety of axes, and have their constituent parts and their uses explained. Those who are really intending to take up climbing or, if they are on a winter course, are probably already committed, will wish to purchase an axe and so it is worth while to detail the points which one would consider when purchasing: length, weight, balance, wood, metal or fibreglass shaft, selection of wooden shafts, cross-section of shaft, ways of improving the grip and the design of the pick and the adze. At this stage it is probably wise to mention the ways of carrying an axe so that it is not a danger to others and the situations in which one would use the various methods, i.e. strapped on the sack when it is not likely to be required quickly, thrust down between the rucksack and the back or carried in a holster when being used intermittently and carried for short distances under the arm with the pick resting against the back of the upper arm on ground where it is being used frequently.

There is some controversy as to whether the axe should be carried pick forward or back when held in the hand. Those who favour the pick forward claim that if one falls on to the axe one stands a greater chance of injury if the pick is to the back. The other argument is that, held with the pick back, the axe is already in the braking position to arrest a slip which may become uncontrolled in the time which it takes to reverse the axe. A little experiment will further show that it requires more contortion of the wrist to hold the pick in such a position that one could impale oneself when the axe is carried pick backwards than when it is carried pick forward. Primarily for the ease of braking it would seem advisable to teach all novices to carry the axe with the pick backward. Once a climber has gained considerable experience of winter work the choice becomes a matter of preference and may be varied to meet particular situations.

If the group is to be taught to belay on snow the ropework involved can be done in a theory session so that the outdoor sessions can be as practical and active as possible. Information on suitable clothing and the equipment which should be carried in the rucksack also needs to be imparted prior to going on the hill.

Practical Work

Terrain: The ideal situation in which to introduce students to the techniques of snow- and ice-craft is a concave bowl of hard-packed snow with a safe, boulder-free run out at the bottom. The occasional protruding boulder can be padded with rucksacks but slopes which have a large number of boulders at the foot should be avoided. If techniques other than the absolute basics are to be taught the slope must be sufficiently concave to give a steep headwall as skills developed to use on steep ground are not easily demonstrated on gentle slopes and the reasons for their use are not immediately obvious. If the slope also has a small ice-boss or if there is one nearby with a good run-out at the foot all the techniques necessary for basic snow- and ice-craft can be practised. Most experienced instructors will usually have several such spots in their own areas where they know that conditions will be suitable at various times during the winter. When walking in winter it is always a good idea to keep an eye open for good locations for future use.

Those who have to travel into a mountain area are often faced with the difficulty of not knowing what the conditions are going to be like and where the best practice slopes are at any particular time. The best solution to this is to have a local mountaineering contact who can be relied upon to give accurate information on conditions throughout the winter.

A good instructor/pupil ratio for basic instruction in winter mountaineering techniques would be 1:4. The limit is 1:8 if much of value is to be achieved in the time available.

Basic Skills

Without doubt the first thing which a novice should know is how to control a slide with his axe. When working in winter, conditions are not always suitable to teach to a set schedule and various aspects of the work have to be introduced when conditions are suitable. Ideally ice-axe braking should be carried out on hard snow where a slide would be difficult to control without using the axe but if the right conditions are not available at first and the snow is soft and deep it is still worth familiarizing the group with the basic, face-down method of braking. Soft snow can usually be improved sufficiently for this purpose by sliding down a fairly steep section a number of times to compact a trough. The following notes set out the progressions in an order which could be followed given ideal conditions. As with other aspects of the work this is not the only way in which the subject can be approached but merely one well-tried method.

To teach braking the first slope used should be just steep enough to permit a fairly gentle slide running out on to a flat, boulder-free base where it should be possible to come to rest without any use of the axe. Given this situation it is then possible to take the group up the slope to the point where the braking practice will commence and allow them to slide down without axes once or twice. This usually increases the confidence of the more nervous once they realize that they cannot come to any harm.

Before moving on to the actual braking the instructor should make sure that all have strong bungs firmly pressed on to the spikes of the axes. An ice axe is a sharp and dangerous cutting tool and can inflict serious injuries in an uncontrolled fall. It is probably true to say that more injuries occur while teaching ice-axe braking than in any other basic teaching situation and a number of these injuries can be avoided by the simple precaution of covering the spike of the axe.

Following a demonstration of the braking position and action the group can adopt a braking position on the snow (Pl. 18) and when this has been checked the brake can be released to give a small slide and then replaced. As confidence increases the group will wish to seek longer and faster slides and care needs to be taken to ensure that they do not stray into areas with a dangerous run-out. Teaching points are as follows.

i A good grip of the head, fingers curled over the top, thumb under the neck of the adze.

ii Other hand *covering* the ferrule and spike. Stress why this is necessary for safety reasons. Those with axes which are too long will find this difficult or impossible to do effectively and may have to borrow a shorter axe.

iii Axe held diagonally across the body from the shoulder of the hand grasping the head to opposite hip.

iv Feet spread, toes dug in and body arched to put weight on the head of the axe. N.B. This position has to be varied when using crampons (see p. 108).

v Emphasis on pressing the pick gently into the snow.

The commonest error at this stage is for the arrest to finish with the axe well above the shoulder due to digging the pick in too hard or not getting the body-weight sufficiently over the head of the axe.

When this has been mastered sufficiently to give reasonable control, the arrest from a slide on the back may be introduced. Further teaching points include the following.

vi Hold the axe in exactly the same grip as before; do not reach out for the snow. It should be stressed that in any falling situation the first reaction should be to adopt the braking position and not to brake until in the correct position to do so.

vii Roll towards the pick, never to the spike. This could dig in causing somersaulting. The roll is best initiated by crossing over the opposite leg to rotate the pelvis and then following it with the upper body.

The common fault at this stage is rolling towards the spike. Once the roll has been accomplished in the prepared position the instructor can position himself part-way down the slope and make the group slide down holding the axe in the air by the ferrule until they reach his position before adopting the braking position.

The next progression is to a head-down slide face-downwards. The problem is to rotate the body into the normal braking position.

viii Hold the axe in the correct manner, stretch it well out to the side at shoulder level to clear the face and insert the pick into the snow. The body will pivot about the pick until sliding feet-down.

ix Remove the pick, bring it into the correct braking position and then commence to brake.

The common fault here is in not removing the pick to regain the braking position before attempting to brake. Head-first slide on the back follows automatically and the method of achieving rotation is basically the same as for the slide on the face except that the pick is more easily placed out to the side between the shoulder and the thigh. Once a feet-first slide has been achieved braking follows as normal. Most people have difficulty getting into a good starting position from which to practise the head-first brakes until they are sufficiently confident to throw themselves down the slope with gay abandon. This can be aided by cutting a big starting platform on which they can kneel or sit as the case may be and, with the instructor giving some support by holding the lower leg, they can then adopt the correct starting position.

These are the basic falling positions but the most difficult of all to control or safely simulate is the tumbling fall. Forward and backward rolls down the slope can give some impression of this but it is generally considered that the backward roll is rather a dangerous undertaking. Done correctly, the climber finishes the roll flat on his face, feet downhill in a nice, easy braking position but it is very easy to land on one of the sharp parts of the axe. The forward roll (Pl. 19) is a much safer proposition and at this stage it is worth while explaining to the group that, using the skills previously learned, they now have the necessary techniques to control any type of fall on snow. They can then be allowed to do a forward roll and attempt to control the fall without any further instruction. This encourages them to think for themselves in a confusing and disorientated (though relatively safe) situation. If the previous stages have been thoroughly practised they should have little difficulty with this and if they are able to control the fall successfully one can have reasonable confidence in their ability to arrest a simple slide in a genuine emergency.

Braking While Wearing Crampons No mention has yet been made of braking with crampons on as this only becomes necessary once people are introduced to cramponning techniques. Practising braking with crampons on is dangerous, particularly in the more difficult situations and it is considered that there is an unjustifiably high chance of injury in this activity. Therefore instruction is usually confined to warning about the somersaulting which can result from trying to use the feet in braking when wearing crampons and the parallel possibility of breaking an ankle. The various methods of braking can be revised with the feet held well clear of the snow but without crampons fitted to establish the necessary technique.

Crash-helmets and gloves should be worn for all braking sessions and waterproof suits will add greatly to comfort. When sliding feet-first it is best to keep the anorak tucked into the overtrousers. Nylon suits are to be preferred as plastic suits have far too little friction which results in fast slides which are difficult to control. This can be turned to some advantage in the conditions mentioned earlier where the snow is soft and it is difficult to gain any speed.

Having mastered the arrest the students will have the confidence to move about the slope without cutting steps and, if the slope is suitably steep, to investigate the limits to which they can take this. At this point the correct methods of holding the axe when traversing low- and high-angle slopes, ascending and descending can be demonstrated and practised. As this follows practice in braking it will readily be appreciated that on slopes steep enough for a slip to occur it is better to hold the axe with the pick to the back (little finger end) of the hand so that it can be brought into immediate use to check a fall.

Step cutting may now be introduced. One of the advantages of delaying step cutting to this point is that if suitable areas of snow are scarce the smooth slope for braking practice is not prematurely destroyed. Once a party of students is let loose on a slope to cut steps it is quickly reduced to a set of craters! The mechanics of step cutting and the main types of step need to be demonstrated before progressing to the techniques of cutting vertically, diagonally, horizontally and downhill.

The main teaching points of step cutting are as follows.

i The axe should be swung from the shoulder, not the wrist.

ii Correct angle of the adze in order to cut without jamming.

iii Rhythmic movement to conserve energy and develop speed.

iv Cut to give a good inward slope to steps for security.

v Cut a large step to change direction or rest.

vi Stand firmly and in balance when cutting.

vii Spacing, not too far apart, particularly if the same steps will have to be used in descent later.

Following the demonstration the students can spread out, to experiment on their own while the instructor moves among them advising and helping where necessary.

Step kicking is a basic skill of winter mountaineering and it may be argued that this is better introduced before step cutting but during the ice-axe braking and immediately following this the group will have been moving about the slope a great deal and will have been kicking steps automatically. Step kicking is a natural action and should require very little teaching. We can over-teach many things and need to consider the merits of each demonstration quite carefully. People can discover the best way to do most things by themselves, given time, and self-discovery is one of the best ways of learning. Things learned in this way tend to be retained more readily. However if this were applied to all things there would be little need for teachers but people would take an awfully long time to educate themselves. The whole point of teaching is that one can pass on many years of hard-won experience in a short time and save much of the valuable but time-consuming self-discovery. Where a thing lends itself to this approach it can and should be used to great effect. Step kicking offers such a situation. Most students will quickly discover the best ways to kick steps up, down and across slopes and it only remains for the instructor to correct minor details here and there. The two points which most frequently require mention are the use of the sawing action of the edge of the boot when kicking sideways and the use of the axe as a support and anchor. Mention needs to be made of the point at which it becomes necessary to cut rather than kick and the point stressed that cutting should not be delayed until one is standing on very small steps as it is easy to be dislodged by the first blow of the axe.

The techniques of belaying on snow and ice and/or cramponning would be the next logical progression but the skills so far dealt with are sufficient if it is intended only that the group should have sufficient expertise to go on accompanied winter walks. At this point a walk involving easy snow slopes would be useful for most groups. Weather conditions permitting much of the newly acquired skill can be brought into use and seen in perspective. Many of the potential hazards such as paths crossing the tops of convex slopes, patches of water ice where the path crosses a stream or gully and cornices can be pointed out.

Inevitably, and usually during the first session, the question of whether or not one should have a sling on the axe will be raised. Expert opinion is divided upon this subject so the only advice which can be given must be based upon the policy of the particular mountain centre or authority, irrespective of what the personal views of the instructor may be. However, as the subject is controversial, if the students are old enough to be able to make their own decisions it is only fair that the matter is fully explained to them along with the reasons for the particular method advocated. Given this information they can evaluate the situation and eventually form their own preferences based on judgement and experience.

For those who may not be entirely sure of the pros and cons of the use of a sling, the main points may be summarized as follows: the main advantage of having a sling of any kind on the axe is that it will be retained if the climber should drop it or have it torn from his grasp during a fall. There are three ways of attaching the sling: a short sling sliding on the shaft, a longer sling attached to the head of the axe reaching to the spike and a very long sling attaching the axe to the body rather than the wrist. All have good and bad points. The short sling on the shaft is attached to a metal slider which is stopped by a small screw just above the ferrule. This screw weakens the shaft, if wooden, and it is claimed that it affects the 'feel' of the axe when testing snow bridges. This difference in feel is negligible and is discounted by most experienced alpinists. The greatest disadvantage is that it is difficult to change hands and that the dangling axe gets in the way when free climbing. This is generally considered to be about the least satisfactory way of securing the axe. The longer wrist sling from the head dispenses with the shaft screw but otherwise is open to the same objections as the short one. They both have the advantage that being on the wrist they are readily accessible and could possibly be regained if lost during a fall.

The long sling to the body allows easy changing of hands but is prone to becoming entangled with other equipment.

The universal disadvantage is that there is a real risk of serious injury if a fall occurs with an axe attached to the body in any way. Those who discard the sling usually consider this to be the overriding factor. The alternative is to carry the axe in a holster where it is easily accessible, easily changed from hand to hand and there is nothing to tangle, but if this method is employed a firm grip must be kept on the axe when in use.

The story is told of the first British party to visit Russia on a climbing expedition. The Russians all had slings on their axes and were surprised to find that the British did not use them. When the Russians asked what would happen if one let go of the axe the reply was 'We never let go of our axes'. About an hour later, at an awkward spot, one of the Britons dropped his axe and the party had to descend some 600 ft (183 m) to collect it. Needless to say there were some rather red faces!

The whole question is a very personal one and each individual must decide which method is best suited to his needs and style of climbing. An exception to all that has been said occurs in the case of steep ice climbing where a wrist loop is essential, not for the above reasons, but for physical support. Most people are just not strong enough to support themselves on two hammer or axe shafts with hands held above the head for long periods.

Further Instruction

Having given students a basis for safe movement in winter, further instruction must be given if they are to progress to winter climbing involving the use of ropes. The more difficult ridges and graded snow and ice climbs necessitate the introduction of modern specialized equipment and techniques, belaying methods, an appreciation of snow structure and its significance for the mountaineer. Good conditions for winter climbing are very dependent on the weather, they just cannot be guaranteed when required and if it is planned to run a course specifically for winter training it is probably best to travel north to Scotland where one can be reasonably certain of finding some suitable conditions between January and March.

1. Belaying Methods

The actual techniques of belaying on snow and ice do not differ from those on rock so far as indirect belaying is concerned. The thing which needs to be explained to the person already conversant with modern rope handling methods is the importance of selecting the best possible anchor in any given set of circumstances. There is a widespread belief that it is not possible to secure good belays when winter climbing and the number of accidents which involve the fall of the whole roped party would seem to bear this out. However this is not true; in some circumstances it is possible to obtain anchors which are every bit as satisfactory as those used in summer. What the accident figures do outline is the need for the average British climber to be made fully aware of modern winter methods of belaying and modern equipment. Most literature on the subject is out of date and those who are not familiar with modern methods are advised to obtain the two publications which outline them clearly: *Modern Snow and Ice Techniques* by Bill March and Eric Langmuir's *Mountain Leadership*.

As it is often necessary to move singly in pitches as on rock the instructor needs to check that the group knows the basic theory of rope handling and, if necessary, to revise this before dealing with the forms of anchor. When dealing with each form of anchor the conditions to which it is best suited and those for which it is not recommended should be given. In some cases the placing of the anchors in relation to the snow and ice and the belayer is critical and should be carefully explained in each case. In particular the 'deadman', the most significant advance in snow anchors for many years, must be placed correctly if it is to be effective. When dealing with anchors their order of merit for different situations should be given in order to give the student a background of knowledge on which to base future decisions. A list of the types of belay used in winter climbing is given below in order of preference.

Natural Rock Belays: Always the number one choice but beware of spikes in gully walls which may be only loosely cemented in by frost or ice. Many gullies are very loose in summertime and a little frost does not materially increase the security of a loose block.

Rock Pitons: As good as natural anchors if properly placed. The danger lies in the fact that the crack into which the peg is placed may well be ice-choked and that the apparently solid peg is biting not into rock but into ice. The best way to deal with this is to hammer in a peg to shatter the ice and then replace it with a larger one if necessary. At least two pegs, preferably in separate cracks, should be used when belaying.

Deadmen: The deadman is the only belay which is suitable for the majority of snow conditions and in well compacted snow it will give a very sound belay provided that it is correctly inserted. The angle to the snow surface is fairly critical. In really soft and powder snow it is suspect but is the only thing yet devised which will afford any security at all.

Ice Pitons and Screws: Although these are listed below *Deadmen* they are not inferior but complementary as neither can be used in situations suitable for the other. Very sound placings of ice pegs and screws can be made but the ice itself is always suspect and the whole area may shatter under shock load. For this reason one should never belay on less than two well placed, well separated, ice screws.

Bollards: Bollards may be cut in hard snow or ice but need to be considerably larger in the former than the latter. Ice bollards are probably better belays than ice screws but are time-consuming to cut.

Snow Stakes and Ice Axes: These are last-resort belays when absolutely nothing else is available and even then should only be used in extremely hard snow. Wooden axes should not be used. Only metal or fibreglass shafts are strong enough to withstand the shock loading of a leader fall.

Direct Belays (Boot/Axe, etc.): These are very specialized and take a great deal of practice to be of any practical value. Definitely not for novices.

Specialist Equipment: The days when an axe and a pair of crampons were the only special equipment one needed for snow- and ice-work are now a thing of the past. The modern beginner is faced with a bewildering variety of sophisticated equipment which will need to be explained

and opportunity provided to handle it. An introduction to this equipment would normally occupy an evening session and during this one
would expect to deal with short axes, curved and pterodactyl axes,
north wall hammers, peg hammers, ice hammers, holsters, rock and
ice pitons and screws, the 'Dead Family' (man, boy and baby!) crampons, correct fitting and methods of sharpening these and survival
equipment. Specialist winter clothing may also be included in this
session or it may be felt that the subject demands a session of its own.
The students will wish to know the purpose of the additional equipment, its usefulness and the points to look for when purchasing. The
actual method of use is probably best dealt with briefly in general terms
and elaborated on during practical sessions.

2. Snow Structure

The theory of snow structure could occupy a whole course by itself
but no amount of theory is a substitute for practical experience of snow
conditions when trying to assess such things as avalanche danger. The
theory is best kept to a minimum but the obviously dangerous situations
– cornices, snow bridges, and all potential avalanche situations – can be
dealt with. If possible, practical examples of these should be studied
when out on the hills. Naturally not all these phenomena can be found
at any one time or place but an observant instructor can spot and point
out many things which would go unnoticed by the novice. If there have
been several snowfalls during the season sections cut in suitable places
will reveal the structure of the underlying layers and can be extremely
valuable both to the student learning to recognize snow structures and to
the instructor, who may wish to know whether the slope is safe for a
particular purpose.

3. Practical Work

For an introduction to the use of advanced techniques and more
specialized equipment the terrain described earlier is still quite suitable.
   All the anchors peculiar to snow and ice can be set up and used and
their relative merits can be discussed in relation to the prevailing conditions. It is always entertaining and instructive to get each student to
place a deadman and then for the whole group to try to pull out each one

in turn. Use a long rope for this for when they do come out it is some-times with great force. The same can be done for snow bollards and other anchors and in this way the superiority of a well placed deadman can easily be demonstrated. In the safe run-out situation of the snow bowl the students can pair off and try holding each other on short leader falls with deadman belays. Care should be taken to ensure that the leader slides well to one side of the belayer and that the rope is laid on the snow in such a way that it cannot entangle the leader as he slides.

Provided that the snow is hard, cramponning may be introduced at this stage but is a waste of time if conditions are unsuitable. If it is intended to teach cramponning it is wise to take the first opportunity of good snow conditions. This may mean introducing it very early on or at the beginning of a session while the snow is still hard from the night frost. Students should be encouraged to try to keep all the points in contact with the snow by ankle flexion and walk with a slightly more open stance to avoid catching the crampons in the clothing. If the snow is sufficiently steep, front pointing can also be practised and the instruc-tor can get the group to tell him which is the more strenuous method. The dangers of cramponning in unsuitable conditions should be men-tioned either here or during the theory session.

4. Ice Techniques

With the advent of curved axes and hammers in the last few years ice techniques have been revolutionized. Pitches which once took hours now take minutes in good conditions and movement on ice begins to approach the grace and fluency of that on rock. A far cry from the grim struggle with time and the elements which frequently occurred in the past.

Unless staff are conversant with modern techniques they would be well advised not to teach ice-craft to beginners. Students, particularly those with a rock climbing background, take readily to the new methods but once taught to cut steps and handholds to climb an ice pitch they find it very much more difficult to adapt to the modern techniques.

Introduction to ice-craft is best done on small bosses of ice offering a variety of angle. At first movement on easy angle ice using all down-pointing spikes of the crampons will develop an increasing confidence in the capabilities of the footwear. Most novices find that descent on ice is much more alarming than ascent and are very chary of trusting the grip of the crampon on even very easy angle ice. As confidence increases they can be introduced to front pointing without hammers or axes on steeper ice. They need to be given a lot of encouragement to tap in the points and allow the body-weight to drive them deeper and to stand upright in balance until they realize that it is very similar to standing on small holds on rock and that their feet are not going to slip. The axes should not be brought into use until all are confident for it is crucial that they learn to rely upon their feet and balance for support rather than the axes.

The use of the axes is best demonstrated on a short, steep pitch of about 15 ft (4·5 m) in height with good belays at the top and an easy way down at the side. Ideally this should be wide enough for more than one rope to be set up pulley-fashion so that there is maximum activity. With good belays above the students can be encouraged to experiment and fully test their security when using axes and front points. Common faults are trying to get the picks deeper into the ice than necessary, often resulting in 'dinner plating' (splitting off in plate-shaped pieces) of the ice, and failure to hit straight so that the pick does not penetrate properly. If there are students unoccupied at this stage they can experiment with the insertion of ice screws and pegs on the ice bosses.

Modern methods of front pointing with curved equipment, although vastly superior to the old methods of dealing with ice in the majority of situations, will not be possible in some circumstances, e.g. where the ice glaze is too thin to obtain good purchase with the hammer and axe. Furthermore the leader of a party is often called upon to deal with a short section of ice when out with a party not carrying specialized equipment or even crampons. For these reasons traditional methods of dealing with ice should also be demonstrated but are better left until the students have been introduced to front-pointing techniques or the tendency can be to want to rely on the security of cut hand- and footholds. Methods of cutting steps in ice with and without crampons, sequence of movements when cutting on ice sufficiently steep to require handholds – importance of planning steps carefully and using natural easings of the angle wherever possible, nick handholds, pigeon-hole hand- and footholds and ice bollards should all be practised.

Following the initial experience of advanced snow- and ice-craft the students can extend their experience to easy gully climbs. These can well be introduced before the ice-craft if conditions are suitable. First, grade one snow gullies of a straightforward nature where they can move easily and concentrate on the belay selection. Climbs should be chosen to give a variety of belaying situations which demand the use of varying forms of anchor if possible. It is usually the case that after being introduced to front pointing on ice the grade one gullies present little difficulty and students are soon ready to tackle gullies with short ice pitches. These should be chosen with care. Routes with good belays at the difficult sections and a diversity of classic features, narrows, ice bulges, cornices, etc. are to be preferred. Climbs which are known to contain sections where belays are poor or unobtainable should be avoided even though they may not be difficult.

Leading on Snow and Ice

Leading winter climbs presents similar problems to leading rock climbs. Are we justified in letting students lead? Have we a moral obligation to see that prospective leaders are trained to lead in a controlled environment? In the case of rock climbing we have seen that the answers to these questions depend largely on the amount of time which the student spends at the centre, i.e. how well the centre staff know him and are able to assess his capabilities. When winter climbing, the decisions, though influenced by a thorough knowledge of the capabilities of the students, may also be based upon other criteria.

Most of the easier winter climbs are very safe provided that the condition of the snow is good and that good belays are available. A leader falling on snow will often succeed in stopping or considerably slowing himself before he comes on to the rope. If he does come on to the rope the forces involved are nowhere near so great as those incurred when holding a falling leader on rock. Given plenty of good snow a climber may belay more or less wherever he wishes which means that long run-outs can be avoided and belays can be taken before attempting steeper sections.

Thus, if students are moving well towards the end of the course, I would consider it quite feasible to allow them to lead in selected situations. The main criteria on which to base a decision to allow students to lead may be summarized as follows.

i The students must be showing ease of movement and competence on steep snow and ice.

ii Their belaying must be good.

iii Snow cover must be good, i.e. firm and deep enough to enable students to crampon or kick good steps and to provide good anchors.

iv The climb, or section of climb, should be straightforward and it should not be necessary to make long run-outs in order to reach anchor points.

v Students should only be allowed to lead on ice if the pitch is very small with good belays above and below (preferably rock anchors) and there is a safe, snow run-out beneath the pitch. Long ice pitches are more akin to leading on rock, with all the attendant dangers, and it is not normally possible on short courses to get sufficient insight into a student's personality to allow him to lead in this situation.

Control over the leading situation can be obtained in two ways. The obvious way is that in which the student leads seconded by the instructor. Although this gives maximum security to the aspirant leader in the event of a fall the instructor is unable to check belays until he joins the leader. On easier snow climbs obtaining a belay is often one of the main difficulties for the inexperienced and it is extremely valuable for the instructor to be on the spot when the belay is being made. In order to achieve this two students may climb as a team on a route which is known to be straightforward and the instructor then soloes alongside. This is obviously only suited to those climbs which are easy enough to be soloed safely and which would normally be soloed by an experienced climber but where a novice would be put on a rope. Using this method the instructor can maintain contact with both leader and second, being able to move freely up and down the slope, and is able to check route finding and belaying on every pitch. If the gully is a wide one it is also possible to run two ropes of students side by side with one instructor controlling both groups.

Instructor/student ratios for gully work should be 1:2 except for the above-mentioned situation.

Snowholing and Winter Camping

Many people consider snowholing to be a pure survival technique but given the right conditions it is fun and, as many expeditions to Patagonia have proved, a very sound alternative to camping (Pl. 20). There is no reason at all why snowholing should not form part of a winter mountaineering course if good conditions prevail. Igloos, in particular, demand good snow and if this is available it is worth making use of it. The knowledge gained could be useful and most people find it fascinating to construct an igloo and to spend the night in one.

As most good winter climbing is found high it can be useful to snow-hole and climb from this for a day or two in good conditions to save the slog to and from the valley each day. Winter camping can also be utilized in the same way. Camping on snow is specialized and even experienced summer campers will find it a completely new experience to camp in winter conditions.

The amount and variety of work outlined above would require a course of more than one week's duration if all were to be completed satisfactorily. As winter conditions are so variable it will normally be found best to leave the detailed day-to-day planning until the time and then to plan the work to make best use of the existing conditions. When engaged upon winter work instructors must be prepared to arrange alternatives at short notice as conditions change rapidly in most parts of the British Isles. A warm, wet wind and rain can quickly reduce perfect conditions to slush.

Chapter Seven

Camping

Camping is complementary to many outdoor activities. Mountaineering, canoeing, caving and cycling are all facilitated if combined with camping which offers freedom from the pressures of civilization and the restrictions of time. It is of course possible to camp as an end in itself, perhaps to get youngsters out into the country, or to face them with a situation where their comfort depends largely upon their own resources and effort. Valid though these reasons may be, most people involved in outdoor activities regard camping as a means to an end. Such ends may be a remote cliff, a lightweight expedition across an area of wild mountain country or a base from which to carry out a number of activities.

When mountaineering ceased to be the preserve of the wealthy, mountaineers had to find a way of living cheaply in the hills. Not for them the traditional gatherings at the classic hotels – Pen y Pass, the Wastwater Head and the like – but barns, bothies, boulders and tents. In seeking economy they learned to live with the hills and were quick to see the advantages of mobility and close proximity to their objectives. Now camping is the accepted norm and the serious climber who operates from a hotel is a rarity. Every weekend hundreds of young people come from the cities to camp in the hills, whatever the weather, and pursue their various interests. The skills of camping are second nature to them and the tent virtually a second home.

If a tent is to be used as a base in all weathers and all seasons the camper has to be able to make himself completely comfortable in any circumstances. Any fool can camp in squalor and discomfort but it requires skill and experience to live in the mountain environment and remain happy, comfortable, warm and well fed over a period of time in bad conditions with only a tent for shelter. Our aims then, in camping, should perhaps be twofold: to give children and others an awareness of the potential of camping as a key to greater enjoyment of the outdoors, and secondly to impart the practical skills necessary to living in the outdoors. We may also have other aims such as the development of self-reliance and confidence. Many youngsters never have to cook even the simplest meal at home and take food, shelter and warmth for granted. They probably never think about these things until they are thrown upon their own resources in the camping situation. However, the first two aims are, I feel, the fundamentals. The others will follow if we concentrate on these.

An initial camping experience should be a satisfactory one because, as in many other things, first impressions are important. Students who return demoralized from a sleepless, wet night are not so likely to display as much enthusiasm as those who have had a dry and enjoyable camp. It is impossible to control the weather but careful choice of site and bad weather alternatives coupled with thorough preparation and training will ensure the best chances of a successful outcome. The following notes should form a guide to the work which one would expect to cover prior to the first expedition.

1. Tents and Tent Erection

i The types of tent available should be covered, e.g. frame, mountain, etc., and a brief comparison and a detailed description of the tent to be be used given, illustrating the points of advantage for the purpose in hand.

ii The principles of erection – this should preferably be a practical demonstration covering the following points.

a Assemble the poles and get the pegs ready.

b With the door fastened peg out the base of the tent to the shape of the groundsheet and with the back into the wind. If there is no wind place the back to the direction from which the bad weather normally comes.

c Untie all guys.

d Fit the poles.

e Erect the back, which will be held against the wind by the guys, and then the front.

f Make sure that the tent is upright and that the ridge is straight.

g Peg out the corner- and then the side-guys, making sure that they are in line with the seams.

h Check for creases denoting uneven strain and adjust the tension of the guys to rectify.

i Put stones on the snow valance where fitted. These should preferably be smooth ones placed well clear of the wall fabric.

iii Pegs and Guys.

a Pegs at right angles to guys.

b Ways of dealing with poor ground: cairns on pegs, guys looped around log held down with stones, guys tied to rocks and well padded. Use of ice axes or deadmen in snow conditions. Cross pegging in sandy soil.

c Make use of the length of the main guys leaving a little for adjustment. This puts minimum strain on the pegs. Side-guys are best adjusted to continue the line of the seam to which they are attached.

iv Striking and folding. Stress the importance of striking when dry if possible and cleaning of groundsheet and pegs.

2. Choosing a Campsite

Points in order of importance for a mountain camp:

i Shelter: boulders, walls, stands of trees (camp in the lee, not underneath), ridges.

ii Dry ground: avoid hollows and marshy-looking places. Look for marsh plants in the grass when dry.

iii Water: good, clean supply close at hand. Streams above habitation are usually safe but check for dead sheep, etc. upstream.

iv Level ground: free from bumps, remove stones and other sharp objects.

v Flat ground: difficult to find on mountains so have head slightly uphill for preference, avoid pitching tent across slope.

3. Living in a Tent

To be really comfortable and at home in a tent requires experience in order to establish a routine and get used to moving around in cramped quarters but a lot of information can be passed on to the novice which will give him a good basis and help him to avoid many of the more obvious mistakes. Living in a tent in dry, sunny conditions is easy; we have to train people to cope with bad weather. The following points are all important and should be dealt with in detail.

i Avoid all unnecessary movement in and out. Collect water before going into the tent and secure the bucket.

ii Avoid touching the sides or, if there is a flysheet, pushing the tent against it or the fabric will leak. Be careful when moving about inside and do not sit side by side.

iii If erecting in rain do not expose areas of canvas until necessary. Work quickly to get the tent standing and shedding water and handle by the guys. As soon as the tent is standing put the rest of the equipment inside. Deal also with problems of packing wet tents.

iv Remove wet clothes in the entrance and store in a polythene bag.

v Keep a dry set of clothes for wear in the tent. Put the wet ones back on when going out for the day.

vi Do not unpack things until required, especially the sleeping bag.

vii Always remove boots before entering the tent.

viii Emphasize the use and value of flysheets.

ix Arrange things systematically, i.e. one corner for food and dixies, the other for stove, matches and candles; personal equipment at the sides and back.

x Cooking inside the tent. This is a must in the mountains for most of the year and one must come to terms with the fire risk by taking sensible precautions.

    a Keep the stove close to the entrance and in a central position in order to keep the flame well away from the walls.

    b Do not stand the stove directly on the groundsheet. Place a flat stone underneath or, if possible, turn the groundsheet back, making sure that the stove is not too close to the doors.

    c Peg out or otherwise secure the doors firmly so that the stove is shielded from draughts which may blow the flame on to the canvas or blow the doors themselves on to the flame.

    d Never try to fill the stove while it is still alight. If using a gas stove the cylinders must not be changed inside the tent, or in the proximity of a naked flame.

    e Do not leave a tent with a stove or candle alight in it.

    f Remove pans before pumping.

    g Hold the pan with a handle when stirring.

    h Remember that a tent is highly inflammable and can burn down completely in under a minute (Pl. 21).

xi Lighting. Candles give the best illumination but again beware of fire. Make sure that the candle is stuck firmly to a heavy tin or fitted in a holder. Beware of falling asleep while reading with a candle alight. Make sure that the candle is well clear of the walls.

xii Insulation. Most of the cold when sleeping comes from the ground.

The most effective insulation is provided by a closed cell, foam mat. This need only extend from shoulder to hip and the lower body can be insulated by the rucksack and spare clothing.

xiii On sloping ground sleep with the head uphill.

4. Stove Lighting

Whatever type of stove is used the students must be completely familiar with the way in which it works, how to light it and how it is controlled. Plenty of practice in a controlled situation is necessary before any attempt is made to light stoves in a tent. Teachers should be thoroughly familiar with the type of stove in use, know what common spares to carry, be able to recognize faults and effect on-the-spot repairs.

5. Food

A group of novices going out to camp for the first time need only know what food they will be taking and how to prepare it. The teacher should know what the food requirements are for the proposed activity and be able to work out a menu which will provide the correct number of calories. The following information is therefore given for the benefit of the teacher.

The body utilizes food to produce heat and other forms of energy, for growth and repair and to maintain body efficiency. The standard unit of heat energy is the *calorie* which is defined as the heat energy necessary to raise the temperature of one gram of water by one degree, e.g. from 15° to 16°C. Dieticians and the medical world usually work in *Calories*, also known as large calories or kilocalories, one Calorie being equal to 1,000 calories.

The energy which is obtained from food is used by the body for two main purposes.

i To maintain the bodily functions, i.e. circulation, breathing, heartbeat, etc. The amount of energy liberated in maintaining these functions when the body is warm, in a state of complete mental and physical rest and has been without food for 12–14 hours is known as the *Basal Metabolic Rate* (B.M.R.).

ii To carry out muscular work. This can be subdivided into the general movements of everyday living such as walking, eating, climbing stairs, etc. and the major activity of the working day.

The B.M.R. of an average-size man is in the region of 2,000 Calories per day but this is affected by a number of factors such as age, sex, race, emotional state, climate, body temperature and the circulating levels of certain hormones. The B.M.R. of women is slightly less than that of men.

As energy cannot be created or destroyed but has to be converted from one form to another a calorie intake equal to the energy output is necessary. If the calorie intake is less than the energy output the body looses weight and if it is higher energy is stored (mainly in the form of fat) and the body gains weight. To balance the basal output the average adult must ingest about 2,000 Calories per day. The calorie requirements above this for normal activity and work will depend on the activity of the individual. For example a person engaged in a sedentary occupation will only require about a further 500 Calories per day whereas a manual worker may require as much as a further 3,000 Calories per day. The amount of energy used is proportional to the surface area of the body, therefore women require slightly fewer calories per day than men. Children require fewer calories overall but more in relation to their size to meet the demands of growth. The following figures relating to the Calorie requirements for moderate activities are taken from the National Research Council of the U.S.A. recommendations for daily dietary allowances 1964.

	Age	*Weight*	*Calorie Requirements*
Men	25	154 lb (70 kg)	2,900
Women	25	128 lb (58 kg)	2,100
Boys	12–15	98 lb (44 kg)	2,000
Girls	12–15	103 lb (47 kg)	2,500

A hard mountaineering day can be classified as fairly heavy manual labour which requires 300–350 Calories per hour. If we consider an eight-hour working day the Calorie requirements would be calculated as follows.

Maintenance of bodily processes: approximately 2,000 Calories
Eight hours' normal activities: approximately 350 Calories
Eight hours' strenuous activity: 2,400–2,800
———————
Calories

Total: 4,750–5,150
Calories

The nutritive value of the food will depend upon how the diet is balanced. This will depend to a certain extent on taste and also financial considerations but the daily intake of protein, fat and carbohydrate should be approximately proportioned as follows: protein, one gram per kilogram of body-weight; carbohydrate, approximately 50–55 per cent of the total daily intake; and the remainder fat. We also require vitamins, salt and various trace elements to remain healthy over a long period. On expeditions of only a few days' duration it is not necessary to worry about vitamins nor the amount of protein intake. It is however important to provide a variety of appetizing food to maintain the required calorie intake which should be divided approximately as follows for a long, arduous day.

Breakfast:	1,300 Calories
Lunch:	1,200 Calories
Evening Meal:	1,200 Calories
Snacks:	1,250 Calories

The actual number of Calories required will of course vary according to age and sex, ambient temperature and the nature of the proposed expedition.

The body is unable to absorb all necessary calorie requirements at one time, especially if energetic activities are to follow and so the intake must be divided and supplied at regular intervals during the day to keep up the reserves of energy. Students should be encouraged to eat a good, hot breakfast before a day on the hills, even if they are not used to doing so, in order to provide a substantial part of the day's calorific requirements.

The weight of normal food in a daily intake is around 6 lb (3 kg) but this can be reduced to about 2 lb (1 kg) by the use of specialized lightweight, dried or concentrated foods. The main disadvantages of dried foods are that they are expensive, they are often inconvenient to prepare (they sometimes require soaking before they reconstitute, for example) and unless well prepared are not as appetizing as fresh foods. If food for several days has to be carried to a high camp or on a long walk weight is going to be important and the diet will perforce be biased towards specialized lightweight foods. For an introduction to camping this is not necessary and it pays to provide foods with which the children are familiar, introducing the minimum of dried foods such as soup, instant potato and dehydrated peas which may already be reasonably familiar to them. Tinned foods which are pre-cooked and easy to prepare are acceptable on introductory and short-term camps of one or two days where expense, familiarity and ease of cooking may be more important considerations than weight and bulk. Contents can often be removed from their tins and sealed in polythene bags thus saving weight and helping to solve the problems of waste disposal.

6. Cooking

Those with no experience of cooking need to be convinced that there is nothing very mysterious or difficult about preparing simple meals. It is important that everything is explained carefully and in detail and preferably children should be given the opportunity to practise cooking indoors before a first camping session. It may even be necessary to explain how to boil water and make tea. When asked, most people will not admit their inability to do such a simple thing but I have, on more than one occasion, checked on the cooking at camp to find one pair with a pan of cold water on the stove and a handful of tea-leaves floating in it!

If possible anything which is at all complicated should be demonstrated. It does not take very long to prepare a sample portion of dried potato for example and to pass it round for all to have a taste. To see it done and know that it will taste good when finished will really boost the confidence of the novice. Children tend to be notoriously conservative regarding food and will view anything new or out of the ordinary with great suspicion. It is therefore important that they are convinced about the ease of camp cooking and the palatability of the finished product. When at camp they should have a hot meal in the evening and at breakfast and they will not do this if they do not like the food or have no idea how to prepare it.

Dangers of fire, scalds and burns should be mentioned and the precautions against these dealt with as detailed in section 3 of this chapter. Flame control for efficiency when cooking should also be stressed. Most beginners tend to be rather afraid of the stove, particularly when the fire hazards have been stressed, and will try to boil water on a really low flame thus making the preparation of a meal a slow and tedious business. The teacher should endeavour to develop group confidence in the use of the stove so that they are not afraid to pump hard when the occasion demands but are also quick to lower the pressure when the need arises, especially in the event of a malfunction. Frying in tents should be discouraged for several reasons. Fire danger is increased, it is difficult to prevent the tent walls being marked by fat splashes and the high-temperature fat can cause severe burns if spilled.

7. Hygiene

Waste disposal, human and otherwise, is the principle concern of camp hygiene. The days of 'Put it under/behind a boulder' are long gone. The pressure of campers on most areas of the British Isles is now such that camping parties must be extremely careful about waste disposal if the whole of the countryside is not to become one vast slum. The answer for tins and other fairly indestructible items is really quite a simple one. If you can carry it in full you can quite easily carry it out empty and throw it in the bin when you get home. The exceptions to this rule are few, particularly in the context of one- and two-day camps. Even if one is being supplied with further food from time to time the rubbish can be handed over at the pickup point. If it is absolutely unavoidable that rubbish must be disposed of on the spot, paper etc. should be burned and tins should be beaten flat, burned to remove all traces of food which might attract animals and also to hasten the rusting process by destroying the tin-plating, and buried deeply. Weight and disposal problems may be simplified by decanting the contents of tins, if suitable, into polythene bags before leaving on expedition and sealing the bags with a hot iron and protective, greaseproof paper or a proper sealing tool.

Excreta should be buried in the topsoil where the bacteria can quickly break it down. Standing camps of more than a few days' duration should have a latrine pit but this must not be too deep. It is preferable to have shallow pits of around 18 in (46 cm) deep and renew them more frequently than to have a really deep one extending into the subsoil. When filling in, the turf, which should have been preserved, must be replaced. Overnight and lightweight expeditions should carry a small digging implement, a gardening trowel is ideal, and this should be placed where it is available and obvious to all as some people will be too shy to ask for it. Lavatory arrangements should always be well away from the water supply and to the leeward. People should be encouraged to wash their hands afterwards and before preparing meals. A high standard of cleanliness should be maintained at camp, both for health reasons and to encourage the pupils to develop a sense of self-respect. It is very easy to let a camp, especially in bad conditions, become very slovenly and dirty.

When striking camp all rubbish should be collected and a final check made to ensure that the site is immaculate. With children one must ensure that every match and small piece of silver paper is picked up in order that they may develop good habits in this respect. If tins have to be carried out a check should be made to ensure that each group has them and that none has been pushed behind boulders, etc.

8. Rucksacks and Load Carrying

There is no reason why students need to be told anything about rucksack design prior to going to camp. They only need to know the best way in which to pack the sack which they are going to use. However, it will be necessary to discuss types of rucksack and their design at some stage in their training and so it could well be introduced at this point if convenient to do so.

In mountain countries as far apart as the Himalayas, Alps and Andes one can see the indigenous people carrying loads on their heads or in very similar, V-shaped baskets. This design has been evolved completely independently over the centuries by the people of each area as being the best way in which to carry a heavy load and the basic principles of modern load-carrying methods and rucksack design are founded on the experience of these mountain people.

For a teacher or instructor a sound coverage and explanation of the basic principles will pave the way for discussion and an understanding of load packing as well as a sensible look at the wide variety of rucksacks and frames. The following may form a simple basis on which to develop ideas for an initial talk or demonstration prior to the practical application of load carrying on an expedition.

Basic Principles
i Try to get the centre of gravity of the load as close to the body as possible.
ii Keep the load high and have the weight pressing downwards through the spine as much as possible. Remember the graceful Hindu lady with the water chatty on her head, or the Billingsgate porter with his load of baskets? This is not very practical for load carrying over great distances or on rough terrain. Parallels can be drawn between the methods used by

mountain people in their daily work to carry a stable load in as near to an ideal position as possible and the ways in which this can be achieved in mountaineering.

iii Pack for good balance and correct placing of the weight, for a good rucksack or packframe can be misused and by bad packing any advantages can be nullified. A badly balanced load can also destroy the enjoyment of the day and can become a danger to balance in exposed situations.

Stress that a badly packed load can be an exhausting load.

In running through load-packing sequences the following points require emphasis and, if there is good preparation beforehand, a splendid practical demonstration can be given as the points are made.

a Items required during the day should be readily accessible and should be left to one side for packing in side-pockets or on the top, e.g. food, first aid, camera, etc.

b If camping, items required on arrival should also be set on one side, e.g. stove and fuel in a polythene bag for a side-pocket, tent and pegs strapped on the top of the sack.

c The lighter equipment such as sleeping bag and spare clothes should go to the bottom of the pack while the heavier equipment is packed from the middle to the top.

d As you pack make sure that the load is well balanced.

e Ensure that food is packed well away from the stove and fuel. It is a good idea to mark one side-pocket and ensure that the fuel is always placed in the same one. Paraffin in particular if once spilled in a pocket will taint food placed there for many weeks afterwards.

f It is useful practice to use a heavy-gauge plastic bag as a liner for the sack which will ensure that you have a waterproof inner. As well as keeping equipment dry on the walk it can make a useful dry store in the tent and, if large enough, will double as a bivvy bag in an emergency. In addition items such as sleeping bag and spare clothes should be packed in individual polythene bags to ensure that they remain dry.

g Avoid having articles hanging on the outside of the sack.

h Having packed the sack, put it on and show the correct method of adjusting waist and shoulder straps for comfort and to prevent the pack swinging.

If the equipment is available a variety of frames and packs can be shown to the group or a series of coloured slides can be prepared to show a variety of load-carrying equipment and some of the common packing faults. The points which need to be mentioned with regard to types of sack are as follows.

Expedition Sacks: Deal with both framed and frameless. Stress the value of waist straps, quick fastening and quick release straps, broad side pockets, long flap and so on. I do know of several mountaineers who have dispensed with the extra weight of a large flap by ensuring that all packing is done in a 500-gauge polythene bag and that the top of the sack closes tightly on draw-cords. However, if you do have a flap ensure that it is big enough to go over an extended load and that the straps are long enough to fasten in this instance.

Packframes: These are a development from those frames used by many primitive peoples such as the Tibetans and the North American Indians. Probably the best known of these was the Yukon packframe devised by the gold prospectors in the Yukon to carry awkwardly shaped loads. The great advantage of a packframe is this ability to accept any type of load, box, bag or implement. The frames can be made from a variety of materials such as wood, fibreglass, alloy tubing, etc. (Pl. 22). The better frames on the market at present tend to be made of light alloy tubing and are extremely comfortable to use but a simple frame can be made in the craft shop for school use out of marine ply at small cost. Almost any sack or old kit-bag can be used in conjunction with the frame. Sacks designed to fit can be bought or made quite easily and cheaply from proofed nylon which is both light and durable in addition to being waterproof if the seams are properly treated. It is a useful feature if the sack can be removed and used as a day sack when at camp but this may cause design problems and additional expense.

Climbing/Day Sacks: These too can sometimes be used for short, lightweight expeditions if carefully packed. There should be no side-pockets and extra straps should be fitted for carrying ice axe and crampons as well as a strong top 'D' ring for sack hauling. A reinforced base is an advantage and a light, sewn-in bivouac extention can be useful.

On short expeditions it should not be necessary to carry enormous loads. It is a good maxim that the total load should not exceed one-third of the body-weight and for young people rarely should a load need to exceed 30 lb (14 kg). If only one member of staff is accompanying a camping group his load will necessarily be considerably heavier than that of the group members as he has nobody with whom to share the equipment and in addition has to carry extra items, e.g. first aid kit, repair kit, trowel, rope, etc. If the group is a strong one some of this communal gear can be divided among the members.

9. Preparation for Camp

When camping equipment is issued it should be stressed that it has to be treated with respect and that it must be returned in the same condition that it was issued in. One of the biggest tasks which confronts any organization teaching outdoor activities is the management and care of the equipment and only if high standards are demanded and adhered to will any measure of success be achieved.

Immediately after the kit issue each camp group should check their equipment to make sure that all is in working order and that tents are complete with pegs, poles and guys. After checking and packing the teacher will need to examine the packs to ascertain whether they have been correctly packed and the weight divided evenly. If a room large enough for the whole group to pack together is available this is useful for it enables the teacher to keep an eye on the packing while it is actually in progress and to give help where needed. Often children have difficulty in getting everything into the sack, usually because they do not succeed in packing all the available small spaces as they progress, with the result that the sack has lots of folds and unfilled corners.

School parties with plenty of time before a camp can benefit greatly by having an overnight camp on the school field. This gives an initial experience of handling the tents, familiarizes the group with pitching and striking and sleeping out without complications in a controlled situation and selected weather conditions.

The Camp

On arrival re-emphasize the points to look for when choosing a site for the tent, pointing out the obvious bad places and then let the groups pick their own sites. While this is going on keep an eye open for people pitching on sites which you know to be unsuitable. It is valuable to know a site which you are using for teaching purposes quite well. If you have seen it in really bad conditions you will know the places to avoid, which are not always obvious even to the trained observer. One useful tip: make sure that your own site is a really good one. If anyone gets rained or blown out in the night you may end up with them in your tent, therefore yours should be secure and dry. If you know the site it pays to stand where you intend to pitch while telling them about siting the tents and then you do not lose your chosen site in the rush!

When the tents are up go round and check to see that they are well pitched, that pegs are well in and that if boulders are being used on a snow valance they are not touching the side-walls.

Keep a careful watch on the cooking – quite a few will need help even if it has all been carefully explained. Inevitably there will be stove lighting troubles, the cause of 90 per cent of which will be insufficient preheating of the burner.

Running a camp is a demanding task and the instructor who disappears for the evening with a book is not fulfilling his duties. It is not easy for most novice campers to know how to occupy themselves in the evenings or in bad weather and again they require guidance. The shorter the days the more difficult it is to do anything as a group such as an evening walk, some boulder problems or stream exploration, etc. and the situation is exacerbated by bad weather when all are confined to individual tents. A prior warning to bring books, cards, etc. will help but the onus is still on the teacher to go round and see that all are happy. This can be a very good time to get to know some of them better, most children will chat quite happily in this informal situation and it is here and in similar situations where experiences are being shared that the seeds of a better classroom relationship are often sown.

Before retiring for the night the teacher should check that all are comfortable. It is particularly important in bad weather to check that pegs are secure, guys are correctly tensioned, no canvas is flapping and that none of the tents has developed leaks. A last check will often save a lot of excitement later in the night.

In the morning get everyone up in plenty of time to get ready. It will take novices a minimum of one and a half hours to cook breakfast and get ready for a day out. Check that all are coping satisfactorily with making a hot breakfast and that they are organized so that one cooks while the other makes the packed lunches if these have not been prepared the previous evening.

When striking camp get all the gear packed before taking down the tents and then ensure that all the groundsheets are cleaned inside. Strike the tents and clean the outsides of the groundsheets before packing. If stones have been used on pegs or snow valances make sure that they are put back where they came from and not left all over the site. See that all rubbish has been collected and have a final thorough group check of the whole area for litter before leaving. Good campers should leave no trace of their presence.

If camping on farmland or other private property do not forget to thank and pay the owner.

On return from camp the group must be briefed on exactly what needs to be done to the equipment. The tent canvas must be thoroughly dried before it is put away and the pegs washed and dried. Any repairs required should be noted and, if possible, done straight away. Stoves should be emptied, cleaned and checked to ensure that all the parts are there before they are put away. Pans should be scrupulously clean and dry. For your own sake set high standards and never accept equipment returned in a bad condition. Your maintenance problems will be less and the equipment will give you longer and better service.

Camping Equipment

Camping has gained a great deal in popularity in recent years and consequently there is a great variety of equipment from which to choose. The following notes are intended as guidance for those wishing to purchase camping equipment.

1. Tents

When purchasing tents it is important to establish what the main use is going to be. Cost is an important and sometimes decisive factor when purchasing any equipment and it pays to ensure that money is not spent on items with unnecessary or undesirable features when a cheaper alternative would do the job as efficiently. When purchasing tents in quantity for group use considerable savings may be effected by choosing wisely and bearing in mind the main use to which they will be put. Mountain tents specifically intended for camping high in the hills, often above snowline, are a waste of money if all the camping is going to take place in the valleys and in summer conditions. If the main purpose is going to be lightweight, mobile camping, a different type of tent will be required from that for standing camps and so on.

The type of tent which is best suited to the purpose is the next factor to be decided. In the lightweight range there are really only two main types: ridge tents and single-pole tents. The ridge tent will stand up better to high wind and there is more room at the highest point. Single-pole tents usually have the length of one side as a doorway which has its advantages in summer but can present difficulties in winter conditions. It has the advantage for mobile camping that, if an outside 'A' pole is used the tent can easily be taken down and packed leaving the flysheet standing. In wet weather this is a great advantage for it means that the tent can be kept dry which will mean less weight to carry and a tent which will not leak at the next stop.

Both ridge and single-pole tents are available as unit tents. Unit tents are sold complete with flysheet and sewn-in groundsheet and are cheaper than tents which can be bought separately. This is because they are always intended to be used complete, the inner tent is normally of cheaper-quality material than the flysheet and it is the latter which provides the weather protection. Tents which can be bought as separate items, on the other hand, are of good-quality material and can be used by themselves. There are many unit tents from which to choose, some of which are good value for money. Important points to consider when buying a unit tent are the quality of the flysheet and groundsheet, the strength of construction and the type and material of the poles. Some unit tents have very heavy steel poles which does not matter if you do not have to carry them far but otherwise alloy poles are to be desired.

Mountain tents, as previously stated, are for high camping. They are 'A' shaped, usually having no side-wall, to provide less wind resistance, which means that the interior is less spacious than a walled tent of the same dimensions. They have 'A' poles sometimes sleeved to increase the rigidity and to enable them to withstand very high winds and a sleeve entrance which is still the best entrance for keeping out driving snow but makes entry and exit more difficult. Another feature is a wide snow valance all round the base on to which snow or rocks can be piled to help to anchor the tent. They are easy to erect and are built to withstand hard usage and fierce conditions but are heavy and very expensive (Pl. 23). Some mountain tents cannot be fitted with a flysheet and, if designed purely for high altitude, may not be waterproof but only snowproof. Ordinary ridge tents are considerably cheaper than mountain tents and the most expensive of these is not necessarily the best. Quite often it is worth while to buy quite a cheap, strongly made tent and modify it to suit one's requirements. Entrances are usually the weak point on cheaper tents and can be improved quite easily by sewing on an extra piece to give more overlap on the doors. A triangular piece sewn on to the base of the door enables it to be pegged out to form a windbreak. A bell end can also be sewn on to the flysheet to protect the back of the tent from driving rain.

The price range and the number of people you will have to accommodate in each tent will also influence your choice of tent. It is worth noting that some unit tents are quite small and one should not judge them solely by the photographs in the catalogues but also compare the dimensions with those of other, known tents. When buying any tent the following points should influence your choice.

Type of Material and Construction: Is the material of good quality? How are the seams made and are they well sewn? Are the 'D' rings strongly sewn on?

Sewn-in or Separate Groundsheets: Most tents for mountain use will have sewn-in groundsheets. This has the advantage of being much more windproof and it is harder for the tent to blow away while you are lying in it! The disadvantage is that the weight of tent and groundsheet cannot be shared and the sewn-in groundsheet adds considerably to cost. For summer camping a sewn-in groundsheet is by no means essential and a cheap and lightweight groundsheet can be made from heavy-duty polythene.

Flysheets: With a unit tent you have to have a flysheet but with other tents it is not absolutely essential. Without a flysheet movement within the tent in wet conditions is severely restricted and in hot weather there is less protection from the heat of the sun. The only disadvantages of having a flysheet are increased weight and bulk and a tendency to be troublesome in high winds. Modern flysheets which come well down to the ground are much less affected by wind than earlier models. Tents tend to be much more weather-resistant in their first year of life. Some people therefore buy a tent, use it without a flysheet until it shows signs of deterioration and then obtain one, thus spreading the outlay over a period of time.

Most experienced campers are of the opinion that a flysheet is essential in the British Isles if camping for any length of time. If mobile camping and wishing to travel light, the fly can be left behind but I have known very successful mobile camps of a week or more in mixed weather where the group has opted to leave the tents behind and just take the flys.

Walls and Eaves: The higher the wall the more headroom there is going to be (and the more wind resistance) but at the same time the roof angle is decreased which reduces its efficiency in shedding rain and snow, the two extremes being the mountain tent with no wall at all, very efficient in wind but rather cramped, and the frame tent with enormous walls and complete freedom to move around which requires a strong steel or alloy framework to give it stability. No hard and fast rules can be laid down regarding optimum wall size as it depends on the tent height and width but the average lightweight tent of around 4 ft (1·2 m) in height will have a wall between 6 and 10 in (15 and 25 cm) high. The higher the wall the wider the eave should be to protect the wall from rain.

Snow Valance: Very useful for high camping and winter camping; not essential for summer valley camping.

Poles: The choice lies between 'A' poles and single poles. Single poles are lighter but take up room in the centre of the tent making entry slightly more awkward, and are much less able to withstand strong winds than 'A' poles. The latter are preferable for all-year-round camping because of the extra stability which they provide. If the 'A' poles are external the tent is easier to erect and strike and if they thread through sleeves stability is again increased. Several tents may now be obtained with a ridge pole which is of considerable advantage in supporting the weight of the flysheet and distributing the load.

Entrance: Ease of access and good ventilation with good closure are the attributes of a good entrance. Zips may appear to be the answer for ease of closure but they do have a habit of breaking at awkward times and can freeze up in winter conditions. The tent must also be pitched very well to avoid undue strain when fastening the zip. Although modern zips are very good and do not give as much trouble as they used to on tents, the sleeve entrance is still to be preferred when camping in winter conditions as it is both snowproof and robust. A good all year round fastening, though not completely snowproof, is the type found on the Blacks Arctic Guinea tent – basically a door with a very generous overlap and external and internal tie cords. This, and any other overlap-type doorway can be further improved by sewing on a length of tape containing press-studs about every two inches (approximately five centimetres). Tape of this kind can be obtained from most large haberdashers. A good feature on a door is a triangular extension on the base so that the door can be pegged out at an angle when cooking. With this as a shelter from the wind it is often possible to cook just outside the tent.

Bell Ends: A bell end is a useful addition to a tent as it provides extra room for equipment and also streamlines the back for better wind resistance.

Pegs and Guys: Alloy pegs are good for lightweight expeditions but are not very well suited to stony ground. Best for mountain use are steel 'Bulldog' pegs in a variety of sizes. Guy-lines should be braided terylene or nylon and should adjust from the tent attachment rather than the peg end as the guy tends to jam in the ground. Mountain tents often have a guy-rope extending right through the ridge for extra strength.

2. Stoves

There are three main types of cooking stove in common use: gas, petrol and paraffin.

Within this range there are many types and sizes, varying considerably in price. The pros and cons of the main types are as follows.

Gas: The gas used is butane, the stove is easy to assemble and quick to light. The boiling time required for one pint of cold water is approximately $6\frac{1}{2}$ minutes. As the fuel gets low the efficiency is considerably reduced as there is no way of increasing pressure. Gas stoves are very expensive to run, and the cylinders may be difficult to obtain in remote areas. Carrying spare cylinders on longer journeys increases the weight more than spare fuel for other types of stove. In very cold conditions the gas will not vaporize unless the cylinder is insulated. Butane gas is highly inflammable and cylinders should never be changed inside the tent or near a naked light.

Petrol: Petrol stoves are compact, light and convenient as no assembly is required. The tall, narrow types are not very stable and the flat varieties are to be preferred. The stove takes about $4\frac{1}{2}$ minutes to boil a pint of water. Petrol is a difficult fuel to carry and store and the stove itself can be extremely dangerous in a confined space if misused. For these reasons it is not really suitable for use by children and novices. The pressure should never be released before the stove has been turned out with the valve key. Nor should this be done near a naked flame.

Normally a separate priming fuel is not necessary as petrol vaporizes much more readily than paraffin but in cold weather the stove will require priming with spare petrol or meths.

Paraffin: The paraffin stove is the cheapest to run, and vies with the petrol stove for efficiency, taking approximately the same time to boil a pint of water. The pressure can be maintained by pumping to give a high flame even when the fuel is running low. The one-pint version is the optimum for size and efficiency. It boils water faster than the half-pint and is not a great deal heavier. The tube burner of the one-pint stove is a more efficient vaporizer than the finger burner of the half-pint and there are less parts to be assembled or lost. They are the only stoves which have folding feet which can be dug into turf or folded to accommodate a slope and give stability. Although assembly and lighting is a little more complicated than on the previously mentioned types of stove the fuel is a very safe one which makes it ideal for use by children. It is reasonable to suggest that the one-pint paraffin stove is still the number one choice of most experienced campers; it is efficient, robust, safe and economical to run. A great number of different makes are available, some much cheaper than others, but one must ensure that it is possible to get spares easily for the cheaper makes.

The time taken to boil water is a measure of efficiency and is important from the point of view of fuel consumption. All the boiling times quoted will be very much increased if the stove is not sheltered from wind and draughts. In winter the stove is used not only to cook but to provide warmth, another reason for using economical and readily available fuels.

The methylated spirit stove is also worth a mention. It has never been successful as a main cooking stove because of the difficulty of arranging a satisfactory flame-control system but can be very useful as a bivouac stove where quick heat for soup or water is all that is required. A very efficient methylated spirit stove has now appeared on the market. Made by Trangia, a Scandinavian firm, it comes as a complete unit of stove and pans which is ideal for carrying in the rucksack for emergencies. The stove is designed to work in wind and is in fact more efficient with a slight wind blowing than in still air. The fuel is the cleanest and most pleasant of all to use and though more expensive than petrol is still much cheaper than gas and the stove is economical in its use. A simmering device is obtainable on some models which would allow simple cooking to be done.

3. Sleeping Bags

Sleeping bags are rather like boots in that quality counts. If you wish to have a good night's sleep in any conditions, buy the best sleeping bag which you can afford. When buying for a group, price will be an obvious consideration but bulk, weight and type of use must also be considered. Ease of cleaning is a secondary factor as all sleeping bags can be dry cleaned but when using communal sleeping bags sheet inners should be insisted upon both for reasons of hygiene and to avoid frequent cleaning. The following points should be taken into consideration when purchasing sleeping bags.

Filling: The type of filling determines the quality of the bag. Down is the best but, because of the sharp rise in price of good-quality down, is very expensive for a good-class bag with a top-quality down filling. Treat with suspicion low-priced bags which claim to have eider-down or goose-down fillings, they won't have. Down/feather mixtures are cheaper but not so warm and rather more bulky. There will, incidentally, be a *small* proportion of small, curled feathers in many down bags. This is supposed to prevent the down compressing too easily under the body but effectiveness is somewhat dubious. A warm bag, designed for winter use will have 3–$3\frac{1}{2}$ lb ($1\cdot4$–$1\cdot6$ kg) of down in it.

At present man-made fibres are not so good as down for fillings although they are rapidly improving. Adequate warmth can be obtained but at a great increase in bulk and weight. The most popular man-made fibre is terylene in batt form which looks just like sheets of cotton wool. Bags made from terylene batt are warm enough for summer use but are bulky for mobile camping. An advantage of terylene batt is that it is quite easy to use when making sleeping bags. One only has to sandwich it between two pieces of the outer covering material, sew it up and quilt it to prevent it from moving within the cover.

Terylene/down mixtures have been tried in order to obtain the advantages of the low compressibility of the terylene for the base and the warmth of the down above. Although the theory was good, these bags have not been successful.

To check the filling of a sleeping bag rub it between your fingers. Down will feel silky to the touch. If feathers are present the stalks can be felt. Stalks have no warmth value, the more stalks the poorer the quality of the filling. Down will also have 'loft', i.e. it will puff up with the warmth of the hand.

Construction: The basic methods of construction are quilting and box quilting with staggered tube and slant box quilting as rather sophisticated variations on the box (Fig. 8). Plain quilting is the cheapest

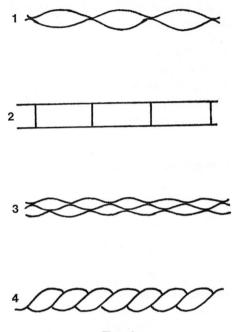

Fig. 8

method of construction and it will be seen from the diagram that where there is a stitching line there is no filling and so no matter how good the quality of the filling this type of bag will always have cold spots. It is, however, a quite adequate construction for a summer sleeping bag if a good insulating layer is used between the bag and groundsheet.

Box quilting eliminates the cold spots by the insertion of a wall between the two layers of covering material so that the filling is enclosed in a series of little boxes. Staggered tube quilting and slant box quilting achieve the same effect as box quilting by ensuring that the stitching lines in the separate layers do not overlap. Any of these methods of construction are suitable for sleeping bags for all-year-round use, the box being by far the most common. To check on box construction take hold of the inner and outer layers of the bag at a stitching line and try to pull them apart. If there is a wall inside they will come apart for the width of this wall, usually about $1-1\frac{1}{2}$ in ($2\cdot5-3\cdot8$ cm).

Some sleeping bags, usually in the higher price range, also have differential cut of the outer and inner covering materials. That is to say that the inner bag is slightly smaller than the outer which allows the down to loft fully without any restriction.

Outer Materials: These can be nylon, terylene or cotton and should be downproof. Cotton is the strongest but also the heaviest and hardest to clean; it is also the cheapest. Nylon and terylene bags are lighter and, the material being smooth, are easier to move around inside but very easily damaged by accidental contact with hot surfaces; stoves, candles, cigarettes, etc.

Fastenings: Zips and other forms of side-opening are best avoided if the bag is for all-year use for, no matter how well constructed, these are always cold spots. A draw-string at the top is useful to narrow the neck once you are inside.

Shape: This is largely a matter of preference. The common shapes available are oblong, usually only found in really cheap bags; tapered; barrel and mummy shape. Tapered bags are widest at the shoulder, narrowing to the foot. They fold up small and are fairly light but movement within the bag is restricted. One tends to move with the bag rather than inside it. The barrel, as the name implies, is widest in the middle. This is a great favourite with climbers, probably from an association of ideas, but it is a very comfortable bag as one is not restricted and can move about within it quite easily. Mummy-shaped bags are named for their resemblance to Egyptian, rather than English, mummies and are designed so that those who wish to sleep with their faces out can still do so and yet have the head enclosed. Mummy-shaped bags tend to be the most expensive as it is the most difficult shape to manufacture.

Care of Sleeping Bags Never store sleeping bags in their stuff bags but open them out and loosely fold them. Keep in a warm, dry place.

If damaged, repair the hole immediately or a considerable amount of down can be lost. The best temporary repair for small holes and tears is

'Sleek' tape which is handy to have in the tent repair kit as it can also be used for groundsheets, tents, etc. If this is not available, sticking plaster from the first-aid kit will do quite well. Try to avoid getting the sleeping bag wet but should this happen dry it carefully and fluff up the down by hand if it has been really wet to stop it sticking in lumps.

After having sleeping bags dry cleaned they should be hung in the open air for a while to ensure that no fumes remain from the cleaning process. These fumes are toxic and have occasionally caused fatalities.

4. Insulation

Most of the cold comes from the ground when sleeping and any sleeping bag will do the job more efficiently if the insulation beneath is good. This can be provided by air-beds, foam, spare clothing or bracken, etc. Air-beds are rather cold in comparison to foams, have to be inflated and have a habit of going down in the middle of the night. They do keep one well above any floods or squalor and pack away quite small. Foam mats require no attention and are warm and comfortable but are rather bulky, particularly the open-cell, egg-box-type mats. These are the most comfortable but soak up water and give drying problems. Closed-cell mats will not soak up water and can therefore be carried rolled on the top of the rucksack if space is a problem. Spare clothing and bracken can supplement any of the above insulators or, if weight-saving is more important than comfort, can be used by themselves. Whatever the type of mat or air-bed chosen it is only necessary to have one which extends from shoulder to hip. These are the points where greatest pressure occurs and where one will experience most cold and discomfort. The lower body can be insulated by the rucksack or clothing, and clothing may also be used for a pillow.

5. Other Equipment

Dixies, mugs, plates, etc. are largely a matter of choice. It is worth buying good-quality dixies of heavy-gauge aluminium as they will give long service if well looked after. Always ensure that they are well rinsed after washing as some powders and detergents attack the aluminium causing the characteristic pitting which will eventually form holes. When buying go for the larger sets. It is easy to cook a small amount in a large dixie but it does not work the other way round. The outer dixie should be 3–4 pint (1·7–2·3 litre) capacity. Check the quality of the pan lifters provided and replace them if necessary. The worst are the alloy ones which grip the rim of the pan and rely on hand pressure. Many potentially dangerous spillages occur with this type, usually when pouring. One of the most efficient is the 'Peter Pan Pot Lifter'. Despite the comical name this ingenious device will lift heavy pans with or without beaded rims and the heavier the pan the better the grip. Unfortunately I believe that this lifter is no longer in production but some are probably still to be found in the shops.

Cups and plates should be unbreakable. Avoid the very light, flexible plastics which tend to taint the food. The same remark applies equally to water containers. One-gallon canvas water-buckets pack away easily and do not affect the taste of the water but tend to be unstable. A very useful item is the toaster. Not only does it provide toast but it also throws the heat down thus warming the tent more efficiently. The best toasters are those which lie flat on the stove and consist of a flat piece of tin with a wire mesh on top. These can be home-manufactured from old biscuit tin and wire mesh and, if this is done, an improvement on the purchased article is to make the toaster round so that there are no sharp corners for packing.

The best candles for tent use are not the long burners seen in camping shops but carriage candles. These are slightly longer than long burners and almost the same diameter so they stand up well. They are considerably cheaper and last almost as long. If only ordinary, long candles can be obtained cut them in half to make them more stable.

It is not necessary to spend money on food containers. If you have a friendly local chemist he will save a great variety of screw-top alloy drug tins and plastic containers for your use which would otherwise be thrown away and which are ideal for sugar, tea, etc.

Chapter Eight

Adventure Activities

I must admit to thinking long and hard before including the word 'Adventure' in the title of this chapter as it is open to much misunderstanding. Despite the dictionary definition we all have our own personal ideas of what constitutes adventure. In his book, *Adventure Education and Outdoor Pursuits*, Colin Mortlock defines adventure as ' . . . a state of mind that begins with feelings of uncertainty about the outcome of a journey and always ends with feelings of enjoyment, satisfaction, or elation about the successful completion of that journey. . . . The initial feeling of uncertainty of outcome is fear of physical or psychological harm. There can be no adventure in Outdoor Pursuits without this fear in the mind of the pupil. Without the fear there would be no challenge.' (Colin Mortlock, *Adventure Education and Outdoor Pursuits*, private publication, printed by F. Middleton & Sons, Ambleside, 1973.)

From discussions about adventure with a number of people it becomes obvious that adventure is a very personal thing and that some people would produce definitions which are at variance with that given above. Many would agree that fear or, perhaps, apprehension is a necessary factor; others would not equate adventure with fear at all. To some, learning to roll a canoe is an adventure; to others, to be a novice at the helm of a sailing dinghy in light winds assisted by an equally inexperienced crew is an adventure. Tom Price, in his article, 'Adventure by Numbers', sums this up very well when he says, 'The truth is that in one important sense, adventure, however much it may be concerned with physical conflict and danger, is really of the mind. What is an adventure to some, may be, to others of more prosaic nature, an ordeal, or an imposition, or a nuisance, or a calamity, or even simply a bore. For just as beauty is in the eye of the beholder, adventure is in the mind and spirit of the adventurer. It is not risks and desperate situations that make adventure, so much as adventurousness.' (Tom Price, 'Adventure by Numbers', *Mountain*, No. 38, September 1974, p. 17.)

Perhaps then, before proceeding, I had better clarify the terminology and state what I mean by 'adventure activities'. Adventure activities, for the purposes of this chapter, are those activities which do not fall into any convenient pigeon-hole such as climbing or walking but which embody aspects of a variety of outdoor activities and demand the application of a number of the relevant techniques for the outcome to be a success. These activities should involve and inspire feelings of excitement, challenge, stimulation, apprehension, pleasure and satisfaction (though not all of these may be found in any one activity) and should be such that, by their nature, they totally involve the pupil both physically and mentally.

One cannot have a planned and controlled adventure, even within the dictionary definition of 'an unexpected or exciting experience, a daring enterprise'. It is the unexpectedness and the uncertainty of outcome which create a real adventure situation. So-called adventures which are deliberately undertaken are neither unexpected nor is the outcome uncertain. The children know that they are going to do something exciting and, whatever their fears or apprehensions may be, they also know that the person in charge is there to see that they come to no real harm. The word adventure, where it is applied to outdoor activity courses in the following text, can be taken to mean a controlled experience involving the previously mentioned factors of excitement, challenge, etc.

There is no doubt that we all have a natural desire to do adventurous things at some time in our lives. In children and adolescents this desire is particularly strong. Their natural curiosity and desire to explore their physical limitations leads them to seek out challenging situations. In a recent television programme young criminals, both male and female, when asked how they came to be involved in crime nearly all put forward as one of their reasons excitement, the thrill of pitting their wits against a challenge, in this case that of the law and society. If such needs are not met in other ways some youngsters will obviously satisfy them by anti-social behaviour. With increasing maturity the majority of people lose or subdue their adventurous inclinations often, sadly, because they feel that society expects it of them, that there is a behaviour pattern to which 'grown-ups' must conform. Henceforth they settle down into comfortable respectability and mediocrity and gain their adventures second-hand from television or through the exploits of others. The more enlightened few retain their sense of adventure throughout life for as Tom Price says, 'The true adventurer takes life so seriously that he

cannot bear to fritter it away on mere comfort and safety and respectability.'

It is not without significance that many of those who retain this zest
for life are devotees of some branch of outdoor activities for the very
essence of these pursuits is that whatever the age and standard of the
performer he can still enjoy them to the full. Unlike the traditional
games player who ceases to play when he leaves school or college, unless
good enough to play for a team, the outdoor enthusiast, whether climber,
walker, cyclist, canoeist, etc., can carry on his chosen pursuit for life. He
does not necessarily compete with others but with himself, and declining
years have no adverse effect upon the enjoyment and satisfaction which
he derives from so doing. The degree of commitment and uncertainty
of outcome is exactly the same for the man attempting a 'Very Difficult'
rock climb who knows his leading limit on rock to be 'Difficult', as it is
for the man attempting an 'Extreme' who leads to 'Very Severe'.

Outdoor pursuits, provided that they are presented in the right way,
offer all the opportunities for self-discovery and challenge which an
adolescent needs. If his imagination is captured he will, in many cases,
gain more than a sport, he will gain a way of life. If the aim of education
in its broadest sense is to equip people to lead full and happy lives as
useful members of the community, outdoor activities, used wisely, can
be powerful weapons to aid the achievement of those aims. A person
who can retain his sense of adventure through the years should be in a
position to offer more to the community than one who quietly stagnates.

Within the field of outdoor education we should seriously consider
whether the 'conventional' activities, such as climbing, walking, canoeing, etc., offer in themselves opportunities which fulfil the needs and
expectations of students. Obviously the needs of the person wishing to
attend a mountaineering or rock climbing course because of a prior
interest in these fields will be well catered for through a conventional
approach to activities but what of the adolescents who comprise school
outdoor activity groups and include the majority of students passing
through L.E.A. centres? What does the fourteen-year-old hope to
experience when he or she goes on an outdoor pursuits course? In the
majority of cases there will be no previous experience of the activities
although they may have been seen on television or may have been discussed with other children from a previous course. The ideas of the
activities will probably be very vague in the minds of most children but
they will, in all probability, be expecting to have some form of exciting
and adventurous time. Without doubt children find some of the

conventional activities dull and meaningless, particularly if they are not presented in an interesting manner. Hill walking, for example, can easily be a dreary plod which leaves the pupils footsore, weary and with a distinctly unenthusiastic outlook towards mountains in general. Even rock climbing, which should be a really stimulating experience, can fail to inspire if the children spend more time listening and standing around than actually climbing.

If we watch the activities of children at play the basic skills are running, jumping, crawling, climbing, swinging, rolling and sliding. If water is available they will paddle, balance on stones, skim stones on the surface and build rafts. In the right surroundings they will build dens and in all cases they will explore, investigate and try out new things. How many of these activities are incorporated in conventional outdoor pursuits and how much use do we make of them? Is it possible that the activities are too skills-orientated, failing to take into account the needs of the pupil? A whole variety of activities can be devised which aim to exploit and extend these basic abilities which all children possess and which also incorporate many of the skills of rock climbing, walking, camping, canoeing, caving and other activities. The advantage of such activities lies in the fact that they do not necessarily require any very specialized terrain or equipment, nor do most of them need to have the very high staff/pupil ratios which one needs for such activities as rock climbing. They can also provide the mental stimulus, challenge and self-reliance which the pupil needs if he is to become totally involved.

The possibilities for adventure activities are bounded only by the imaginations of the teachers concerned. Any area of open country can offer a variety of possibilities which will fire the enthusiasm of a group of schoolchildren. The basic ingredients for a reasonably flexible situation are trees, rocks and water, things which can be found within short travelling distances of most towns within the British Isles.

Quite a lot of imaginative and unconventional work has been done with children in some areas, often with a great deal of success. Staffordshire Education Authority began to run Adventure courses for older schoolchildren at their Coven Camp School some fifteen years ago. These were planned and executed by Les Williams, the warden at that time, a man of great imagination who had a real insight into the sort of activities guaranteed to stimulate adolescents, arouse their interest and capture their imaginations. The school consisted of a wooden hut in a large field containing a small area of woodland, within which were some swampy pools, and bounded by a canal. Not a very exciting area at first glance and the school was not overendowed with equipment but what they had they really used to great advantage. A brochure was sent round the schools, not aimed at the staff as most brochures tend to be, but at the children, offering them an adventure course and posing questions such as 'Have you ever cooked an egg in an orange? Can you light a fire twenty feet up a tree?' When the children came on the course it was noticeable that the brochure had appealed to them and fired their imaginations because a lot of them brought the brochures with them and made sure that they did everything which was listed. Boys would come up to members of staff towards the end of the course and say 'I have not cooked an egg in an orange yet.' So off they would go armed with egg, orange and instructions to find out about it, to discover for themselves, surely one of the keys to adventure.

Very little work of a conventional nature took place on the ten-day course and instruction was kept to the minimum necessary to achieve the aims of the course. Even a conventional instruction session was likely to take an unconventional turn and develop in ways totally unexpected to the children. The school ran a house system, four houses each gaining points in competition for a trophy which changed hands according to points score each evening. When the group were introduced to stove lighting each house worked in a corner of the hut assembling and lighting the stoves (paraffin) under supervision. After this the stoves were put away under the house tables and some other activity was undertaken. Some time later the warden would switch out all the lights, shout 'Ten house-points for the first house with all its stoves lit and a pint of water boiling', then he would grab a fire extinguisher and stand by. Surprisingly he never had to use the extinguisher.

The unexpected was the order of the day. While practising tying a clove hitch each group would tie a hitch to the wrist of the next person so that they formed a circle. When all groups were tied in this manner the warden might tell them to go over the climbing-frame and back or again, perhaps, light a stove. There were rope courses over the pools in the woods, groups competed to build monkey bridges and commando bridges and get themselves across or would perhaps be asked to get the whole group across the canal without getting wet and be given an assortment of equipment to do so. The whole course aimed at keeping the group on its toes from the moment it arrived until it left. They soon realized that anything was likely to happen and that it paid to listen and do what they were told. Quite early on in the course, for example, they would be asked to build bivouac shelters in the woods for house-points and would be given some basic ideas on the subject then left to their own devices for the afternoon. Naturally quite a few fooled around in the woods and did not produce very good shelters but nothing was said, the points given and the bivouacs forgotten until bedtime when it would be announced that as a special treat they were going to be allowed to sleep in their shelters. This always caused some consternation among the ones who had not worked very hard as they were thrust out into the autumn night (adventure courses were always in the autumn term) but their attention level was noticeably improved thereafter!

Some rock climbing was done but with a lot of concentration on abseiling, and some canoeing on a small, local rapid. Both of these activities involved very little instruction, the emphasis was on action. Each course culminated in a three-day scheme which was always held in a mountain area and usually took the form of an elaborate sort of game with one half of the group perhaps posing as smugglers with an objective to gain and the others as customs and excise men out to stop them. They had two camps in different places usually, carried all their equipment, did a lot of mountain walking (and running), and never found it boring. In fact it did not occur to most of them that they had been mountain walking. It was interesting to observe the reactions of boys to work of this kind. They came expecting something exciting and they found it. It would take around two days for them to adjust to what was happening and then they were ready for anything. They did not get much formal instruction but they climbed, walked, camped, navigated, canoed, handled ropes and all the time were deeply involved in what was going on.

Colin Mortlock, while warden at the City of Oxford centre in Glasbury, was another person who saw the needs of children as not being compatible with the accepted mountain or water activity course and set out to offer them adventure. Working with a larger number of staff possessing a higher degree of technical expertise in an area of much more varied terrain (large rivers such as the Wye and Usk close by, gorges, caves and the Breacon Beacons), Mortlock's approach was somewhat different to that of Les Williams but again had the needs of the pupils as the basis for the courses and achieved the same kind of results. A lot of use was made of the rough sections of the river with inflatable dinghy trips in flood, river crossings in which the main object was to end up very wet and canoe trips. Caving provided novelty of surrounding and unusual terrain and gorge exploration gave opportunities for difficult rock climbing in safety above pools of water, boulder hopping, ropework and balancing activities. The course would travel away from the centre to the coasts of Gower and Pembroke where they would make sea-cliff traverses and participate in a number of other activities which made the best use of that area such as traverses of rocky foreshores, involving boulder hopping and balancing and sand-dune jumping.

An important difference between the course run by Les Williams and that run by Colin Mortlock was that the latter had more activities which in themselves could have been dangerous and which took place in potentially dangerous situations. To be able to do this in safety and with complete control over the situation demanded an alert staff with a great deal of expertise in mountain, water and caving activities. I have detailed the work of these two centres to emphasize the point that they both made full use of their local resources, both in the way of natural facilities and of staff and equipment, and they each worked within the capabilities of the staff. Both courses achieved things which many conventional courses fail to do. They set challenges, extended children to what they thought were their limits in order that they might discover new limits and gain more self-confidence, and above all they gave enjoyment, excitement and a desire to do more and explore further.

The activities which can be used to create adventure situations are numerous and will depend a great deal on the terrain available and its imaginative use. Pl. 24 illustrates one example. Many centres and individuals are now introducing some adventure activities into their programmes. Gorge exploration is very popular where suitable terrain exists. There is something exciting about being in a gorge, a feeling of true exploration which has an instant appeal to most youngsters. Once inside, each gorge has its own peculiar atmosphere and obstacles and no two are alike. Many gorges have sections from which it is not possible to escape quickly or easily and care should be taken to find out how high and how quickly the water is likely to rise during a period of heavy rain. Teachers contemplating gorge exploration with school parties should have an awareness of possible hazardous situations and should be familiar with rock climbing techniques and rope handling methods which may be necessary to safeguard certain sections. Before taking children into a gorge, prior inspection is essential to establish areas of interest and also of potential danger and to seek the answers to questions such as the type and amount of equipment which will be required, escape points and suitability for non-swimmers. In this situation as in sea-cliff traversing it is often advisable to equip weak swimmers with buoyancy aids. Gorge exploration, like caving (with which it has a certain affinity) can be a very wet business. Hot drinks should be carried and a change of clothing should be readily available on completion of the journey.

Caving, although a conventional activity, presents children with an adventurous situation without any need for detailed instruction beforehand. Total darkness, unusual surroundings and exploring with a headlamp is sufficient to make any caving trip into an adventure for most children. Colin Mortlock was well aware of the adventure potential of caving and made full use of it on his course at Woodlands. However, it cannot be too strongly emphasized that any party going into a cave must be accompanied by an experienced caver and at least one other competent adult. Accidents have been known to occur to inexperienced parties in even the simplest cave systems. In areas where there are no natural caves there has been a tendency towards mine exploration as a substitute. Anyone contemplating this should be extremely careful as the dangers in old mines far outweigh those of caves. Many mines were only kept safe by constant maintenance and once work has ceased they rapidly become most unsafe. In wet mines any timbers which support roofs, etc. soon become rotten and there is a great danger of rock falls. Loose ladders and shafts covered by rotting planks are further hazards and there are others. Unless it is possible to be absolutely certain that a mine is safe do not go there with parties.

In parts of North Wales old slate quarries offer other unusual activities and can be fascinating places to explore but again there is a necessity for care. Make sure that you know precisely what you are undertaking. Anything man-made, old and on the grand scale is likely to have dangers, not all of which will be obvious.

Snow can provide endless opportunities for adventure activities. Sliding immediately springs to mind and can offer a variety of exciting variations such as sliding on or in a large polythene bag or any of these things head-first. Most sliding activities can become completely uncontrolled so the run-out must be gentle and boulder free. If there is sufficient snow, expeditions involving snowholing or building igloos are worth trying provided that the temperature is low enough to keep the snow firm.

The need for a high degree of competence among staff for adventure activities is perhaps greater than that required for more conventional work. Pl. 25 shows one reason why. Vigilance, imagination, awareness, concentration and technical skill are vital requirements for people undertaking such work. Situations where everyone tends to be involved at once such as gorge exploration and sea-level traverses need efficient organization to ensure that the group does not get strung out to such an extent that students are engaged on two difficult sections at the same time with only one member of staff to supervise. As in all things connected with the outdoors, know your limitations and those imposed by the weather and terrain and stay within them when working with young people. It should, however, be recognized that staff ineptitude can limit the natural development of the pupils and in this situation one should be prepared to obtain help from people with more experience.

A final word on adventure. The work portrayed has been wholly child-based but much of it holds equal fascination for adults if they can be persuaded to shed some of their inhibitions. A party of young adults, on a wet day, exploring the possibilities of a smooth slab of rock with a muddy puddle at the base in terms of sliding, running up and down and jumping has to be seen to be believed.

Qualifications in Mountaineering

Apart from the Guide Certificate, issued by the British Mountaineering Council, which is not intended to be a teaching qualification, all qualifications for those wishing to instruct mountaineering or take parties into mountainous areas of the British Isles are governed by the Mountain Leadership Training Boards of England, Scotland and Northern Ireland. The qualifications which may be obtained are as follows.

i The Mountain Leadership Certificate (Summer) (M.L.C.)
ii The Mountain Leadership Certificate (Winter)
iii The Mountaineering Instructor's Certificate (M.I.C.)
iv The Mountaineering Instructor's Advanced Certificate (M.I.A.C.)

The requirements for these certificates, as stated by the M.L.T.B. in its pamphlets, are as follows:

I. The Mountain Leadership Certificate (Summer)

The certificate covers basic training in the skills required to take a party on walking and camping expeditions in mountainous areas of the United Kingdom under normal summer conditions. It is intended as an essential requirement for teachers, youth leaders and other adults wishing to take young people on to the mountains and to show them how to enjoy their mountain walking with safety.

The certificate, which is valid throughout the United Kingdom, will be awarded to individuals who fulfil the requirements of the scheme to the satisfaction of the Board. An annual list of Introductory Training and Assessment courses approved by the Board is available on request.

1. Introductory Training Requirements

i Attendance at an approved one-week residential course of introductory training. (A series of at least four weekends, each of two full days' activity may be accepted by the Board as equivalent.)

ii Completion of a period of training, during which practical experience of mountaincraft is obtained and recorded in an official log-book. This may be purchased from the secretary of any of the Boards (see Appendix 2).

1. Log-Book Experience

In gaining experience between introductory training and assessment the candidate should record in the log-book at least sixteen days in mountainous country, half of which is to involve overnight camping. Candidates are also advised that they should have climbed thirty named peaks of 2,000–3,000 ft (600–900 m), selected from more than one mountainous area, in the care of other more experienced climbers.

Experience in leading and instructing small parties of novices under the guidance of a more experienced leader in steep hill country is advised.

Every opportunity should be taken of practising the skills learned at basic training, i.e. map and compass work, campcraft, etc. Further practice in rock climbing should only be taken under expert guidance.

Special note will be taken of any expeditions which the candidate has carried out in winter conditions, also any help that may have been given at search and rescue operations. Candidates are expected to conform to the points listed in the *Country Code* and the *Mountain Code*, and are recommended to take a more than average interest in the countryside.

3. Assessment Requirements

Having fulfilled the training requirements the candidate will be tested, during a one-week residential course, in accordance with the 'Syllabus Requirements', and if found to be proficient in all sections, the course director will submit a report of recommendation that the Board should award the candidate the Mountain Leadership Certificate.

4. Bibliography

All candidates should be conversant with the following: *Mountain Leadership Handbook, Safety On Mountains, Mountain and Cave Rescue, Country Code* and *Mountain Code*.

5. *Age Limits*

The minimum age limits for entry and the award of the Certificate are as follows.

i To enter an introductory training course, eighteen years.

ii For assessment of the Certificate, twenty years.

6. *First Aid Requirements*

Before being awarded the Certificate, all candidates must hold a currently valid Adult Certificate in First Aid (of the British Red Cross Society, St. John's/St. Andrew's Ambulance Associations or the Armed Services First Aid Certificate).

7. *Exemption*

Persons who are already experienced in leadership of groups in mountainous districts may apply to the Mountain Leadership Training Board to be exempt from attendance at an introductory course, and from the period of log-book experience. Candidates must in this case be able to provide a fully completed log-book covering the 'Syllabus Requirements'.

8. *Syllabus Requirements*

I. Map and Compass

i Map Scales.

ii Conventional Signs.

iii Map References – the grid.

iv Methods of showing relief.

v Contours – description of ground from information on the map.

vi Topographical features.

vii Measurement of distance.

viii Calculation of speed of movement over varying terrain with and without loads – Naismith's Rule.

ix Setting of the map – without compass.

x Navigation across country with map but no compass.

xi Types of compass.

xii Methods of obtaining grid and magnetic bearings.

xiii Plotting a compass course from the ground and from the map.

xiv Method of obtaining a position fix by resection (back bearing).

xv Navigation across country with map and compass especially in poor visibility (e.g. at night).

xvi Hints of natural wayfinding (e.g. use of sun or stars).

xvii Methods of teaching simple map and compass work to beginners.

II. Route Planning
i Choice of route.

ii Preparation of route cards.

  a Bearings.

  b Distances covered.

  c Time taken.

iii Selection of campsites.

iv Expedition rationing.

v Escape routes.

vi Bad weather alternatives.

vii Sources of aid (telephones, M.R. post, etc.).

III. Walking Skills
i Individual skills – pace, rhythm, foot placing, conservation of energy, balance and co-ordination.

ii Party skills – leader and tailman, psychology of the group, corporate strength.

iii Party procedure on different terrain, e.g. scree, narrow ridge, steep broken slopes.

IV. Personal Equipment
Personal equipment required for mountain expeditions, both high- and low-level and in *all* weather conditions. Information given should stress the effects of wind, temperature and humidity as well as providing information on design construction and types of material, care and maintenance of equipment.

V. Camping Equipment
i Knowledge of the use of different types and makes of the following.

  a Tents.

  b Sleeping bags.

c Stoves.

d Rucksacks and other lightweight camping equipment.

ii Knowledge of the principles of packing and loading personal and communal equipment.

iii Care and maintenance of camping equipment.

iv Knowledge of items required on given types of expedition, e.g. high-level/low-level, long- short-duration camps.

VI. Camp Craft

i Camp organization and siting.

ii Tent organization and siting.

iii Camp daily routine.

iv Hygiene on camp.

v *Country Code.*

vi Camp foods and cooking.

vii Use of mountain huts and bothies.

VII. Security on Steep Ground

The small amount of rock climbing included in the course is not intended to train leaders as rock climbers. Its purpose is to familiarize candidates with elementary techniques, to enable them to appreciate the limits of what should be attempted by a party without rock climbing experience, to recognize difficulties and potential dangers of terrain, and to give competent help in cases of emergency. Any safe method of rope management will be accepted at Assessment, but the method used and taught should involve the use of the rope alone. It is emphasized that the techniques advocated here are not necessarily those which would be suitable for rock climbing. The following points will be dealt with.

i Practice of movement on rock.

ii Ropes and rope management. Tying on: figure of eight on the bight; waist belay with gloves; belaying and interchange of belay; moving together.

iii Decision-taking on steep, broken ground. Route selection, roping up, choice of belay, negotiating loose rock, etc.

iv Use and limitations of hillwalking safety line: 120 ft (36 m) of No. 2 laid rope or 7 mm or 9 mm kernmantel rope.

v Use of rope as a handrail and for linking party together.

vi Abseiling with safety rope.

VIII. River Crossing
When and when not to ford rivers followed by practice in the following.
i Methods of finding the best crossing points.
ii Methods of crossing with and without line.
iii Skills and safety precautions to be practised by the individual – methods of progression, use of 'third leg', procedure with a pack, reduction of resistance or friction, danger from trees and snags.

IX. Special Mountain Hazards

Exposure
i An understanding of the causes of the condition known as 'exposure' or 'hypothermia'.
ii Recognition of the signs and symptoms exhibited by 'exposure' cases.
iii Awareness of the basis for prevention of 'exposure'.
iv Awareness of the methods for treatment of an 'exposure' case
  a In the field.
  b At base.

Frostbite: An understanding of the condition, its signs, symptoms, prevention and treatment.

Lightning: An understanding of the probable distribution of strikes on a mountain, and of the probable flow lines of resulting ground currents.

Heat Exhaustion: An understanding of the condition, its signs, symptoms, prevention and treatment.

X. Weather
An elementary knowledge of weather, for example the following.
i Interpretation of the weather map recognizing
  a Areas of high pressure.
  b Airflows (e.g. northerly airstream).
  c Depressions and frontal systems.
  d Weather normally associated with (a) (b) and (c).
ii Major cloud forms and associated weather developments.
iii Sources of information on weather, e.g. newspapers, radio/television broadcasts, R.A.F. stations.

XI. Accident Procedures

Candidates must have practical ability and theoretical knowledge in depth of the following.

i Procedure in the event of an accident.

ii Methods of search and evacuation.

iii Equipment contained in M.R. posts and boxes.

iv Improvised mountain rescue equipment – application and limitations – rope seats, rope stretchers, sleds, ski stretchers.

XII. Details of Clubs, Organizations, etc.

i Details of organizations providing training in mountain activities.

ii Details of clubs, etc. willing to accept young people as members.

iii Guide-books, etc.

XIII. Responsibility of Party Leader, etc.

A thorough knowledge and awareness of the function and responsibilities of the party leader (see section III).

XIV. Additional Interests

A mountain leader should be knowledgeable about some or all of the following subjects: geology, flora and fauna, local history, history of mountaineering, photography, etc.

II. The Mountain Leadership Certificate (Winter)

The Mountain Leadership Certificate (Winter) provides training in the very exacting skills required for taking parties on to the Scottish mountains under winter conditions. It is intended primarily for candidates for the Instructor's Certificates, for whom it forms an essential part of the training requirements, but it is also open to those who, having gained the Mountain Leadership Certificate (Summer), seek this particular qualification only.

To lead a party into the Scottish mountains in winter conditions is a serious undertaking. Demands are made on the leader which are far in excess of his normal responsibilities in summer. For this reason, only competent all-round mountaineers with experience of winter climbing will be likely to satisfy Assessment requirements.

Courses at mountain centres, valuable though they are, require to be supplemented by personal experience over a considerable period. Quite stringent requirements are, therefore, laid down in this syllabus.

1. Requirements

i Candidates who apply for Assessment must hold the Mountain Leadership Certificate (Summer).

This requirement does not apply absolutely to registered candidates for the Mountaineering Instructor's Certificate Schemes for which there are special conditions.

All candidates, however, must hold a currently valid adult certificate in first aid (of the British Red Cross Society, St Andrew's/St John's Ambulance Associations or the Armed Services First Aid Certificate), as required for the Summer Certificate, which *must* be presented at Assessment.

ii The scheme of training, experience and Assessment will be conducted on the same lines as that instituted for the Summer Certificate. The following must be completed to the satisfaction of the Board.

A. Basic Training Course lasting at least one week or four weekends at a centre approved by the Board for the specific purpose of staging training for the Scottish Mountain Leadership Certificate (Winter), e.g. Glenmore Lodge. *A weekend will consist of two full days' activity.*

B.1. Candidates are required to gain practical experience of winter climbing over a minimum period of two seasons, one of these in Scotland or in a major mountain range abroad, e.g. the Alps, and to have experience of differing types of snow conditions.

B.2. Candidates are required to present a detailed record of expeditions and experience which will be recorded in a personal log-book. This log-book is in the form of a ring-back folder capable of holding log-book inserts for all the Board's schemes and is normally issued at the Basic Training Course. All Assessment candidates must present a fully completed log-book to the Director *at the commencement* of the week of Assessment. Candidates may purchase a log-book at any time from the Secretary.

B.3. Candidates may find it to their advantage to attend appropriate courses, e.g. Snow and Ice Climbing, Winter Survival, Mountain Rescue, etc. Details of such courses available in Scotland may be obtained from the Secretary.

C. A residential period of Assessment, lasting at least one week, at a centre approved by the Board. (At present Glenmore Lodge is the only centre approved to stage Assessment of candidates.)

iii All candidates are required to be conversant with *Mountain Leader-*

ship, the official handbook of the Mountain Leadership Training Boards of Great Britain, *Safety on Mountains,* and *The Mountain Rescue Handbook.*

2. Syllabus

For assessment purposes, candidates will be required to be familiar with the theory and practice of the following.

i Carrying the ice axe.

ii Kicking steps up and down in snow.

iii Use of the axe: walking, step cutting up and down, belaying, glissading, probing.

iv Braking, in self-arrest technique.

v Holding a fall on steep snow from above and from below.

vi Step cutting on ice, with and without crampons.

vii Cramponning up and down, and traversing.

viii Belaying on ice – use of pitons and screws.

ix Surmounting a cornice.

x Moving together.

xi Winter climbing at Grade 1 standard.

xii Special equipment (individual and group) necessary for winter mountaineering.

xiii Winter camp-craft.

xiv Construction of snowholes and emergency shelters.

xv Knowledge of the causes, symptoms and treatment of exposure and frostbite.

xvi A knowledge of the development of weather systems in wintertime.

xvii A basic knowledge of the process of firnification and evaluation of avalanche risks.

xviii Winter search and evacuation techniques, including the searching of avalanche tips.

xix A sound knowledge of the planning of winter expeditions and the special responsibilities of the party leader.

3. Exemptions

Experienced mountaineers may elect, in the light of their experience, to exempt themselves from part or all of section B. Exemption from section A and section B should only be considered by exceptionally well qualified candidates. A relevant advisory circular on this point is available from the Secretary. All candidates proceeding direct to Assessment must be in possession of a current Adult First Aid Certificate, together with a fully completed log-book; both documents to be presented to the Director of Assessment.

4. Assessment

i Candidates will be assessed on the basis of their ability to lead others in winter conditions as well as their personal competence in the various skills.
ii The Board will appoint a Director of Assessment to whom shall be delegated the responsibility for making all necessary arrangements.
iii Subsequent to Assessment of candidates, the Director of Assessment will make recommendations to the Board regarding the award of Certificates.

The Mountaineering Instructor's Certificate Scheme

1. Administrative Structure
i There are two grades of certification: Mountaineering Instructor's Certificate, and Mountaineering Instructor's Advanced Certificate.
ii The scheme provides for the training and certification of mountaineering instructors as a progression from and at a more advanced stage than the Mountain Leadership Certificate.
iii Training and certificates are designed to meet the needs both of permanent instructors and of part-time or temporary instructors, whether employed at mountain centres or on the staff of schools, youth centres etc. The arrangements are as follows.

Mountaineering Instructor's Certificate
i All candidates for the certificates, being at least eighteen years of age, will apply for registration with the appropriate Board according to their place of work at the time.
ii Candidates will be accepted as trainees by the Boards if possessing basic qualifications (Mountain Leadership Certificate or evidence of proficiency as certified by the Warden of a mountain centre).

Candidates will be required to pay a registration fee to the appropriate training Board, this sum to cover administrative expenses. Log-books are available from the Secretary at an additional charge.

iii On registration the candidate will record in the log-book mountaineering experience, relevant experience as an instructor or teacher and particulars of training courses attended.

iv To qualify for the Mountaineering Instructor's Certificate the candidate must have covered the syllabus requirements, and must satisfy the Assessors that he is able to give instruction in general mountaineering to all age groups.

v Before being accepted for Assessment, each candidate should usually have attended one general instructor's training course of one week's duration or not less than four weekends or have equivalent experience. The minimum age for attendance at Assessment will be twenty years and application for Assessment will be to the Secretary of the appropriate Board.

vi The training courses will be courses sponsored by the two Boards. They will take place at approved mountain centres and it will be the aim that courses should be offered at various times of the year, both in general and specific aspects of mountaineering instruction; in general courses, at least, particular attention will be given to relevant educational issues.

vii Assessment will take place at either of the two National Mountain Centres or at a centre approved for this purpose by the Boards. Directors of Assessment will be appointed by the respective Boards and they will initiate all arrangements for assessment. In each case the relevant Board will appoint at least two external assessors who will be expected to attend at the centre concerned for all or the final part of the assessment period. Assessment will be based primarily on practical work during the period involving the instruction of students or others at the centre, examination of the log-book and any necessary interviews. The assessment period will be for a minimum of one week. Final recommendations will be formulated at a meeting of assessors at the end of the period.

viii The recommendations of the assessors as certified by them will be transmitted to the Secretary of the appropriate Board, and the Board may either accept their recommendations, or, for good reasons, require the reassessment of the candidate. Once the Board's approval has been given, the successful candidate will be awarded a certificate headed 'Mountain Leadership Training Boards of Great Britain' signifying the grade of the award and signed appropriately.

Mountaineering Instructor's Advanced Certificate
i To qualify for the certificate the candidate must satisfy the following requirements.

a Be able to demonstrate his ability in all aspects of the syllabus at a higher standard than required for the Mountaineering Instructor's Certificate.

b Have held the Mountaineering Instructor's Certificate for at least one year.

c Be able to produce evidence of further experience to the satisfaction of the Boards.

d Attend a residential Assessment of one week's duration at one of the National Mountain Centres or at a centre approved for this purpose under a Director of Assessment appointed by the Boards.

ii The candidate will be given details of the scheme of training and will continue to record in the log-book material relevant to syllabus requirements.

iii The recommendations of the assessors will be submitted to the Board as in Mountaineering Instructor's Certificate.

III. Mountaineering Instructor's Certificate

Assessment Requirements

Before being accepted for assessment each candidate should usually have completed a one-week training course or the equivalent. In addition he must satisfy the Director of Assessment as regards the following:
i Substantial experience in at least three mountain districts, e.g. North Wales, Lake District, Skye.
ii At least twelve hill walking expeditions involving mobile camps or bivouacs, half to have been in the winter months of December to March.
iii Three years' rock climbing experience and the leadership of twenty-five Very Difficult or higher rock climbs, on big cliffs such as Lliwedd, Pillar, Buachaille. (This stipulation has, in the past, given rise to much confusion and is now generally interpreted as 'To have led or led the cruxes of twenty-five Very Difficult or higher rock climbs of over 300 ft (91 m) in length.') These climbs must be listed with dates. A candidate should be able to lead unseen and in poor weather any climb of this standard.

iv A minimum of six weeks (forty-two days) as instructor in mountain-craft on courses recognized by the Board, e.g. at Wardens Association Centres, or special L.E.A. S.C./S.S.C. courses.
v Possession of the Scottish Mountain Leadership Certificate (Winter).
vi Possession of a valid Adult First Aid Certificate.

Syllabus

Candidates will be assessed at a one-week Assessment on their knowledge of the syllabus given below.

Complete familiarity with the syllabus material will be expected. Candidates must be able to speak fluently about all aspects of the work and be able to answer questions to a class. They must show an ability to illustrate the syllabus material from personal experience and to approach difficult areas of teaching in a variety of ways.

Candidates are recommended to become fully conversant with the material presented in *Mountain Leadership*.

Candidates must be able to undertake difficult and strenuous mountain journeys and demonstrate with the ease of long practice the art of navigation in mountains. The highest standards of camp-craft and bivouac techniques will be demanded, and the candidate's ability to achieve comfort in the wildest of situations will be noted.

I. Map and Compass Work: Theory and Practical
i Map references.
ii Map scales.
iii Conventional signs.
iv Topographical features.
v Setting of the map with and without the use of compass.
vi Measurement of distance and calculations of speed of movement on varying terrain – with and without loads.
vii Methods of showing relief. Contours of glaciated country, sections, gradients, intervisibility. The limitations of contours. Reading ground from information on map.
viii Compass – types of compass and methods of obtaining grid and magnetic bearings. Plotting of courses.
ix Practice in cross-country navigation with map and without compass.
x Practice in navigation with compass at night and in white-out conditions.

xi Methods of resection and obtaining position by resection.
xii Hints on natural wayfinding, e.g. use of sun, stars.
xiii The National Grid – its false origin, primary squares and their subdivisions. The difference between Grid and True North.
xiv Organization and control of map and compass exercises and orienteering courses.
xv Knowledge of continental maps.
xvi Knowledge of place names.
xvii A simple explanation of how maps are made and of the earth's magnetic field is often asked for by students, therefore, background reading in these areas is important to an instructor.

II. Route Planning
Choice of route, preparation of route cards and choice of 'escape' routes or bad weather alternatives.

III. Walking Skills
i Individual skills – pace, rhythm, conservation of energy, foot placing, balance and co-ordination.
ii Procedure of party when scrambling or on rough terrain, e.g. scree, narrow ridges, steep broken slopes.

IV. Personal Equipment
Personal equipment required for mountain and moorland expeditions in *all* weather conditions. Information given should stress the effects of wind, temperatures and humidity as well as providing information on design, construction and types of material to look for. Care of equipment and emphasis on personal and group selection of equipment bearing in mind factors such as cost and durability.

V. Camping Equipment
i Examination of equipment and demonstration of use, i.e. stove lighting, load carrying and packing, tents and tent erection.
ii Other camp equipment and advice on suitability and care of equipment. Emphasis on personal and group selection of equipment, bearing in mind factors such as cost and durability.

VI. Camp-craft, Camp Planning and Bivouacking
i Organization of the whole camp and individual tents.
ii Choice of site and siting of tents.

iii Camp foods – cooking and planning of meals.
iv Use of mountain huts and bothies.
v Hygiene in huts, bothies and on camps.
vi Knowledge of the *Country Code*.
vii Use of emergency bivouacs.

VII. Expedition Planning

i Have an understanding of the relevant issues required for the care of young people in the mountains, particularly load carrying capacity and long distance capability of individuals and the maintenance of morale.
ii Ability to plan a mobile expedition in a remote mountain area.
iii Knowledge of requirements of Expedition Section of Duke of Edinburgh's Award Scheme.
iv Ability to plan and control a number of groups, moving independently as on Duke of Edinburgh's Gold Award Expeditions, so that a right balance between adventure and safety is maintained.
v Relation of routes to conditions, weather, terrain, time of year, group size, age, sex, fitness and suitability of group's equipment.

VIII. Weather

i Knowledge of air masses and their properties with particular reference to the four main types affecting the British Isles, generally as airstreams: Maritime Polar (mP), Continental Polar (cP), Maritime Tropical (mT), Continental Tropical (cT).
ii Knowledge of weather associated with anticyclones, depressions and frontal systems (summer and winter).
iii Ability to infer local situations from information given on BBC sound and television programmes, including the BBC shipping forecasts (1500 metres long-wave service).
iv Ability to read a synoptic chart as shown in some national newspapers or on television and to infer local situations from the information given.
v Knowledge of main cloud types and awareness of significant signs indicating weather changes.
vi Knowledge of the significance of barometric pressure and changes in wind direction and in humidity.
vii Knowledge of the effect of altitude and of landforms on weather conditions.
viii Knowledge of the occurrence and significance of micro-climate.
ix Knowledge of the Beaufort Scale, including the symbols used on

charts, the descriptions, the wind speeds and means of recognition, particularly of Force 6 (i.e. strong breeze) upwards to Force 10 (whole gale).

IX. Rock Climbing

i History of rock climbing in Britain – growth of clubs, B.M.C., outdoor centres, M.L.T.B., etc. Development of techniques and equipment.

ii Where to climb in Britain – grading of climbs and guide-books.

iii Organizing a series of indoor rock climbing sessions.

iv Organizing a rock climbing session for four to five beginners on a practice rock.

v Leading and instructing two more advanced pupils on a large cliff climb of Very Difficult standard.

vi Teaching an acceptable rope technique and having a knowledge of various other methods, including artificial climbing. Being familiar with the use and misuse of climbing aids, including slings, pitons, nuts, karabiners, etc.

X. River Crossings

When and when not to ford rivers followed by practice in the following.

i Methods of finding the best crossing points.

ii Methods of crossing with and without line.

iii Skills and safety precautions to be used by the individual, e.g. method of progression, use of third leg, procedure with pack, reduction of resistance or friction, danger from trees and snags.

XI. Mountain Rescue

i Main causes of mountain accidents.

ii The distress signals.

iii Action of party members, e.g. application of simple first aid, the four essentials of information, procedure in exceptional circumstances.

iv Mountain rescue posts, police assistance, R.A.F. mountain rescue, the First Aid organizations and their function in the rescue service.

v Ability to organize a search and evacuation.

vi Knowledge of visual communications.

vii Familiarity with various stretchers, e.g. Thomas, Duff, MacInnes, Mariner and use of Thomas splint.

viii Ability to take part in the evacuation of an injured climber from a cliff using an acceptable method.

ix Knowledge of other equipment, such as types of illumination for night work, radios, etc.

x Mouth to mouth (nose) resuscitation.

xi Improvisation of rescue equipment.

XII. Responsibilities of Party Leader

The skills of party leader should be understood.

i Party leader to choose route, set pace, appoint rear men, ensure the adequate equipping of the party and make all necessary decisions leading to the good conduct and safety of the party. Extra equipment to be carried by the leader.

ii Responsibilities of rear man.

XIII. Special Mountain Hazards

i Recognition and treatment of cases of exhaustion and exposure.

ii Effects of sun and heat.

iii Recognition and treatment of frostbite.

XIV. Law Relating to Access to Land

Knowledge of the Countryside Acts (Scotland and England) and an understanding of the parts played by such bodies as: Countryside Commission, National Trust, Nature Conservancy and Forestry Commission.

IV. Mountaineering Instructor's Advanced Certificate

Requirements

The candidate is required to demonstrate his ability in all aspects of the M.I.C. syllabus at a higher level.

He must also fulfil the following.

i Be capable of leading and instructing to Very Severe standard on rock and leading artificial climbs at grade A2/A3.

ii Have at least three seasons' snow and ice climbing experience and be capable of leading and instructing to Grade 2 standard, in addition to holding the Scottish Mountain Leadership Certificate (Winter).

iii Be able to organize a large-scale search and evacuation.

iv Be able to demonstrate ability to organize the evacuation of an injured climber from a major cliff using acceptable vertical and horizontal lowering methods.

v Have a knowledge of the progressive programming of various mountain activities.

vi Have an understanding of the mountain environment and in particular of one area.

vii Have developed one or more specialist studies related to the mountain environment and produce appropriate evidence of this for assessment purposes.

viii Have an understanding of the relevant issues required for the care of young people in the mountains.

Useful Addresses

1. National Bodies

Mountain Leadership Training Board,
Crawford House,
Precinct Centre,
Manchester University,
Booth Street East,
Manchester M13 9 RZ.

Scottish Mountain Leadership Training Board,
4 Queensferry Street,
Edinburgh EH2 4BP.
(031–225 5544)

Northern Ireland Mountain Leadership Training Board,
49 Malone Road,
Belfast BT9 6RZ.
(0232–669510 669519)

British Association of Ski Instructors,
Miss Hazel Bain,
c/o Coylumbridge Hotel,
Aviemore,
Inverness-shire.

British Mountaineering Council,
Crawford House,
Precinct Centre,
Manchester University,
Booth Street East,
Manchester M13 9RZ.

National Association for Outdoor Education,
Membership Secretary,
'Lundy',
Bishopstone,
Hereford HR4 7JE.

Duke of Edinburgh Award Scheme,
2 Old Queen Street,
London SW1.
(01–930 7681)

Mountain Bothies Association,
40 Maitland Street,
Dumfermline,
Fife KY12 8AF

British Orienteering Federation,
Lea Green,
Nr. Matlock,
Derbyshire DE4 5GJ.

Outward Bound Trust,
34 Broadway
London SW1 HOBQ.

The Schools Hebridean Society,   Nature Conservancy,
15 Julian Road,   19 Belgrave Square,
Sneyd Park,   London SW1.
Bristol.

National Ski Federation of Great
Britain,
118 Eaton Square,
London SW1.
(01–235 8228)

2. Mountaineering Equipment Suppliers

L.D. Mountain Centre,   Joe Brown,
34 Dean Street,   Menai Hall,
Newcastle-upon-Tyne.   Llanberis,
                                        Gwynedd.

Ellis Brigham,
6–14 Cathedral Street,   Helly-Hansen (U.K.) Ltd.,
Manchester 4.   12 Ronald Close,
                                        Kempston,
Moac Ltd.,   Bedford.
Wellington Place,
Liverpool Road,   Mountain Equipment Ltd.,
Manchester M3 4NQ.   George Street,
                                        Glossop,
Ultimate Equipment Ltd.,   Derbyshire.
The Butts,
Warkworth,   Y.H.A. Services,
Northumberland.   29 John Adam Street,
                                        London WC2N 6JE.
Blacks,
Port Glasgow,   Nevisport,
Strathclyde.   131 High Street,
                                        Fort William,
Banton and Co. Ltd.,   Highland.
(Point Five Products),
Meadow Lane,
Nottingham NG2 3HP.

Karrimore Products Ltd.,
Avenue Parade,
Accrington BB5 6PR
Lancashire.

Bryan Stokes,
9 Charles Street,
Sheffield,
Yorkshire.

Arvon's Mountaineering Stores,
11 Ogwen Terrace,
Bethesda,
Gwynedd.

Pindisports,
14–18 Holborn,
London EC1.

Peck (U.K.) Ltd.,
Barnsdale Hall,
Oakham,
Rutland.

Fishers,
2 Borrowdale Road,
Keswick,
Cumbria CA12 5DA.

Troll Products,
Diggle Mill,
Diggle,
Near Oldham,
Lancashire.

Graham Tiso,
13 Wellington Place,
Leith,
Edinburgh 6.

3. Magazines

Mountain Magazine Ltd.,
56 Sylvester Road,
London N2.

Skier,
Holmes McDougall Ltd.,
36 Tay Street,
Perth PH1 5TT.

Orienteer,
18 Doneraile Street,
London SW6 6EN.

Climber and Rambler,
Holmes McDougall Ltd.,
36 Tay Street,
Perth PH1 5TT.

4. Miscellaneous

*National Audio-Visual Aids
Library,*
2 Paxton Place,
Gipsey Road,
London SE27
(01–670 4247).

Pennine Boats,
(For downproof nylon),
Hardknott,
Holmbride,
Huddersfield,
Yorkshire.

Meteorological Office,
London Road,
Bracknell,
Berkshire.

Rallymaps,
(For all OS Maps ready plastic
covered.)
14 Kingston Park,
West Wellow,
Romsey,
Hampshire.

Bibliography

Blackshaw, A., *Mountaineering*, Penguin, London, 1970.

British Mountaineering Council, *Mountain Hypothermia* (Pamphlet). *Mountain and Cave Rescue*.

Debenham, F., *Map Making*, Blackie & Sons, London, 1954.

Department of Education and Science, *Safety in Outdoor Pursuits*, H.M.S.O., London, 1972.

Disley, J., *Your Way With Map and Compass*, Blond Educational, Iliffe, 1971.

Drasdo, H., *Education in the Mountain Centres*, Tyddyn Gabriel, Llanrwst, 1972.

Edholme, O. G., and Bacharach, A. L. (eds.), *Exploration Medicine*, John Wright & Sons, Bristol, 1965.

Fraser, C., *Avalanche Enigma*, John Murray, London, 1966.

Jackson, J. A., et al., *Safety on Mountains*, Central Council for Physical Recreation, 7th edn., London, 1968.

Jones, Dr. T., and Jones, Dr. I., *Some Thoughts on the Organization of Mountain Search and Rescue Operations With Notes on Mountain Rescue First Aid*, Ogwen Valley Mountain Rescue Organization, Bangor, 1973.

Kephart, H., *Camping and Woodcraft*, Macmillan, 22nd edn., New York, 1965.

La Chapelle, E., *ABC of Avalanche Safety*, Highlander Publishing Co., 1961.

Langmuir, E., *Mountain Leadership*, Scottish Sports Council, Edinburgh, 1973.

MacInnes, H., *Climbing*, Scottish Youth Hostel Association, Edinburgh, 1963.
International Mountain Rescue Handbook, Constable, London, 1972.

March, W., *Improvised Techniques in Mountain Rescue*, Private publication, available from S.S.C. Centre, Glenmore Lodge.

Modern Snow and Ice Techniques, Cicerone Press, Manchester, 1973.

Mariner, W., *Mountain Rescue Techniques*, (trans. Trott, O. T., and Beam, K. G.) Oesterreichischer Alpenverein, Innsbruck, 1963.

Meldrum, K. I., and Parker, T. M., *Outdoor Education*, Dent, London, 1973.

Ministry of Agriculture, Fisheries and Food, *Manual of Nutrition*, H.M.S.O., London, 1961.

Ministry of Education, *Camping and Education* (Pamphlet 41), H.M.S.O., London, 1961.

Mortlock, C., *Adventure Education and Outdoor Pursuits*, Private Pub., Ambleside, 1973.

National Parks Commission, *Country Code*, H.M.S.O., London.

Robbins, R., *Basic Rockcraft*, La Siesta Press, California, 1971.

Schools Council, *Out and About*, Evans/Methuen Educational, London, 1972.

Seligman, G., *Snow Structure and Ski Fields*, Joseph Adam, Brussels, 1962.

Young, G. W., *Mountain Craft*, Methuen, London, 1920.

Index